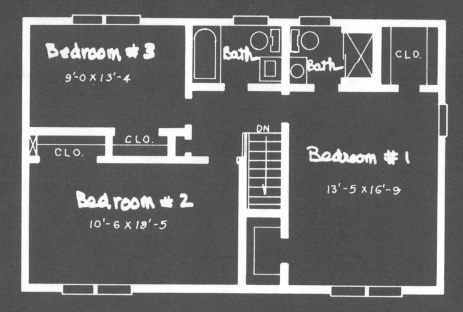

Bedroom # 3
9'-0 X 13'-4

Bath

Bath

CLO.

CLO.

CLO.

DN

Bedroom # 1
13'-5 X 16'-9

Bedroom # 2
10'-6 X 18'-5

Plan # 3 upstairs

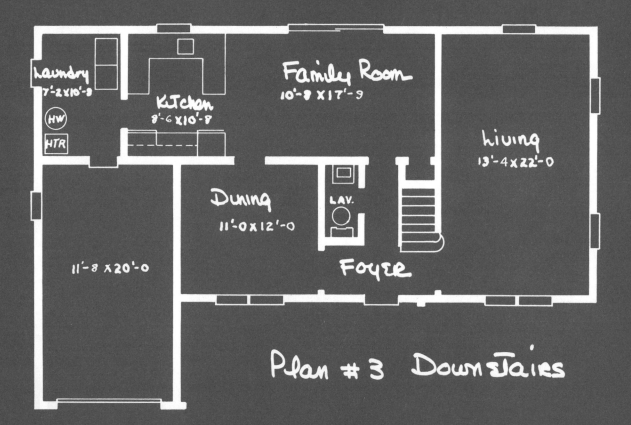

Laundry
7'-2 X10'-8

HW

HTR

Kitchen
8'-6 X10'-8

Family Room
10'-8 X17'-9

Living
13'-4 X 22'-0

Dining
11'-0 X 12'-0

LAV.

11'-8 X 20'-0

Foyer

Plan # 3 Downstairs

THE FAMILY DECORATES A HOME

THE FAMILY DECORATES A HOME

Carleton Varney

THE BOBBS-MERRILL COMPANY, INC.
Indianapolis and New York

Also by the Author:

You and Your Apartment

The Bobbs-Merrill Company, Inc.
A Subsidiary of Howard W. Sams & Co., Inc.
Publishers/Indianapolis · Kansas City · New York

I like to decorate with the colors of a sunny day....

I acknowledge my associates and friends who have worked with me
on this book, on sunny as well as on cloudy days. Thank you for
making even the cloudy days the pleasant ones they truly were:

My associates at Dorothy Draper & Company, Inc.:

Leon Hegwood
Charlotte Sabathie
Brenda Cambridge
William Shirley
Sandra Roberts
Robert Benton
Steven Sabathie
Enid Gulla
Irving N. Fishman
John Melick
Terry Matis
Stuart McGuire
Paula Odellas
Richard Hunnings

My friends in the design and decorating field:

Marjorie Reis
Devorah Buxbaum
Ernest Fox
Bert Bailee
Helene Cantor
Henry Christensen
Hal Rosenstein
Don Spencer
John Reidy
Jack Antman

My literary agent, book-jacket photographer and book designer:

Rosalind Cole
Morton Tadder
Nancy Reeser

My very special and dear friends, both here and around the world:

Joan Crawford
Inge & Kaj Velden
Mary & Tom McInerney
Mimi Uzman
Virginia & Bennie Yeager
Mrs. E. Truman Wright
John Stevens
Joan & Jerry Diamond
Sandra & George Ohrstrom
Hamilton Crawford
Rita Rawley
Babbie & Dennis Coleman
Tom Coffey
Geraldine Sheppard

My friends at Bobbs-Merrill, with whom I have enjoyed working
on this and other books:

William Finneran
Maybelle Brown
Winnie Duncan
Marion Israel
Susanne Conley

My love:

Suzanne Lickdyke

My family:

Mr. & Mrs. Sam Guyler
Amanda Bates Guyler

And my editor, for whom I have the greatest respect and admiration,

Robert Amussen

To the memory of Julia and
Carleton Varney, Sr., my mother and father,
who delighted in the pleasures of home,
this book is lovingly written.

Contents

Chapter IV—The Most Magical Decorating Tool—Color • 82

Chapter V—Ways with Walls and Ceilings • 96

Chapter VI—On Floors and Floor Coverings • 113

Chapter VII—Ways with Windows • 130

Chapter VIII—Furniture: How To Select, What To Select, When To Buy • 153

Chapter IX—Looking at Light: Adding with Accessories • 197

Chapter X—Finally • 210

Chapter I

What Is a Home?

When we speak of a home in this book we mean that single-family dwelling lived in by the family unit, including all immediate members. It is also the dwelling visited, and lived in, on occasion, by relatives. The home is not only enjoyed by the immediate family and relatives; it is also that place where friends are entertained—the parents' friends and the children's friends.

A home is by definition an active place, where toys and coloring books often clutter the floors and where vases of flowers often decorate the mantel. A home is not the same at every moment of the day, nor is it the same at every season, nor are its rooms decorated and furnished in the same manner year after year. Just as a person goes through a number of changes in his lifetime, so does a home. A baby's room does not always remain for baby: a baby grows. So do the character, decoration, and furnishings in his room. A home, to be a home, goes through and accepts change easily and readily. A home is not the model house you often see decorated and fancily trimmed—complete with china in the dining room breakfront and the right color soap in the master bathroom, soap matching the color of the towels. A home, to be a home, must reflect the character of the family, and as that character grows and changes, the decorations and character of a home grow and change as well.

The model houses seen in a number of residential communities today are idea houses. They show a prospective buyer what he can expect in a two-, three-, or four-bedroom home. I have recently been involved in designing, planning, and specifying for model homes in a growing new community. As the decorator/designer, it was up to me to specify kitchen-cabinet finishes and plastic-laminate colors for kitchen counter tops and bathroom lavatory units. I was also called upon to coordinate bathroom tiles with bathroom fixtures, to select and chart paint colors. In essence, my role was to select those "standard" finishes buyers could expect in their homes. In today's growing new residential communities, homes are being built to conform with the tastes and wishes of the buyer. The buyer may like the counter tops in the kitchen of Model Home A, but prefer the kitchen floor tile in Model Home B. Today's residential-community home buyer has the freedom to select the tile from one model and the flooring from another model, provided the tile and floor covering are "building standards." A building standard is a product available in the finishing of any model home. A building standard can be anything used in the home—from a floor tile to a refrigerator to a lavette unit.

If you are a prospective home buyer and are considering a home in a new residential community in which the community developer will build to your specifications, be certain to have all building standards clearly outlined on paper as well as in your mind. I say this because I once was an offender to the cause of the development-home buyer. In decorating some model development homes, I innocently used materials for flooring, wall covering, etc., other than building standards. Prospective buyers then had to be told that certain things—a specific flooring in a dining area, a specific chandelier in an entrance hall, a specific wallpaper in a bedroom area— were not building standards, but decorator choices, the decorator being me! I learned my lesson, and today, whenever I am asked to consult on development homes, I always use building standards in my planning and decorating.

In essence, I try to bring the interior building-standard materials up to a new level. I suggest to the developer/builder new floor patterns, new types of kitchen-cabinet laminates, new lighting fixtures. I suggest the newest materials available, considering, of course, the developer/builder's unit cost structure per material.

When visiting model homes in new communities, be certain you examine building standards. Be careful that the interior decorator has not filled the model with interior cabinets, floor coverings, etc., that you cannot have in your eventual home. Interior decorators often do much with model homes strictly for effect and design, as well as for sales and merchandising value. Make certain you know your building standards!

A home can be many things indeed! It can be a new dwelling in a residential developer's community. It can be a 30-year-old single-family unit in Rockford, Illinois. It can be a home you lay out, plan, and build yourself. Whether it be that house in Rockford, Illinois, or Pickwick, Long Island, or the house you build for the family in Marblehead, Massachusetts, single-family homes have several elements in common within their basic format.

The Case of Up and Down (House Plans #1-#4)

I know a number of families who decidedly prefer the up-and-down staircase home, most often painted white with ebony-black or forest-green shutters. In the case of the two-level house with black shutters, may I suggest a bright-red door! I have always liked a two-level home with black shutters and cheery red front door. There is something crisp about the black, white, and red color combination in exterior as well as interior decorating.

For those who prefer or who live in the up-and-down-stairs home (more often called the two-story or two-level house), I have presented here four different house plans. Plans #1, #2, and #3 have the basic house-design elements in common. Each has a living room, dining room, foyer, family room, kitchen, utility room, and small lavatory/powder room on the first floor. It is with the layout and decoration of these rooms that we shall concern ourselves. We shall also be concerning ourselves with the layout, decorating, and furnishing of the second-floor rooms—namely, the bedrooms. Plans #1 and #2 are similar in that each has four bedrooms. Plan #1 is preferable to Plan #2 in that the master bedroom has a full dressing room/bath area, the bathroom having both a tub and a shower. In Plan #2 the master bedroom has a bathroom area with only a shower; the bathroom with a tub in Plan #2 is shared by three rooms (bedrooms two, three, and four). In this case, Mother, if she wants to take a tub, must use the children's bathroom.

Not installing a tub in the master bedroom suite is an economy situation in this plan. Many community-development homes today are built in this manner—each has one bath with tub and one bath with shower. My advice: when you invest in a development home, put in two bathtubs and two showers. It's a wise investment for your home and especially for family morale.

Plan #3 is a two-story home layout with three bedrooms. On the second floor you will note that the master bedroom has only a shower in the bathroom; the bathtub is located in the upstairs children's bath at the top of the stairs.

Plan #4 is a four-bedroom home with two bedrooms on the main floor and two bedrooms on the second floor. In this plan, the master bedroom shares a bathroom with bedroom four. The family who would select this plan would most likely use bedroom four as a guest bedroom or for a future baby's room. From the plan you will note that bedrooms one and two, on the first floor, occupy space that might have been used as a large family room/kitchen and separate dining room. In Plans #1, #2, and #3, all houses have separate dining rooms and family rooms. Plan #4 must use the area off the kitchen, marked "Dining," as a dual-purpose room, for family breakfasts as well as for more formal family dining. Plans #1, #2, and #3 with their living-kitchen-family rooms are the preferred plans. Most families today like the idea of having a family-type room, be that room off the kitchen or in the basement.

Recently, I visited friends in Illinois for Thanksgiving. The family, two girls and their parents, lived in a single-family dwelling with dining room, kitchen-living room, one bedroom, and bath on the first floor. The father's special pride was his game/rumpus room and bar in the basement. He himself had paneled the wall with $\frac{1}{4}$-inch walnut plywood, and built his own bar, complete with an overhanging shingled roof. Homes with an area for a family room are always preferred, by plan as well as by pleasure. You will be reading about the family room in Chapter IV.

If you contemplate buying, building, or renting a two-story "up and down" house, be on the lookout for the following space elements:

1. Look for a house with a spacious foyer or one that at least has a foyer area. Plans #1, #2, and #3 all have foyer areas that can accommodate, perhaps, a small table, commode, or console. Plan #4 has no foyer area whatsoever. Upon entering the house using Plan #4, you enter directly into the living room.

2. Select a house with a good-sized living room. Rooms ranging from 22 feet to 26 feet in length are quite standard. Room widths can range

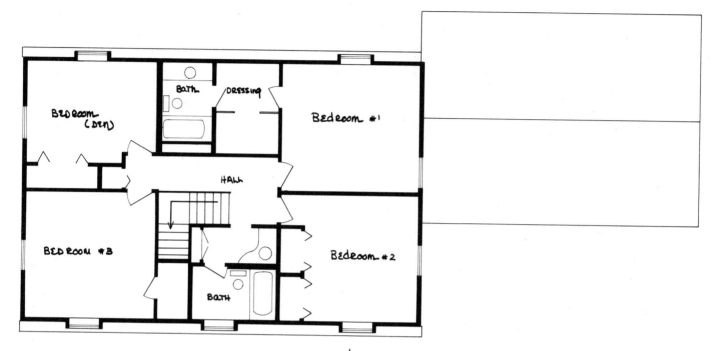

Plan #1 - Upstairs

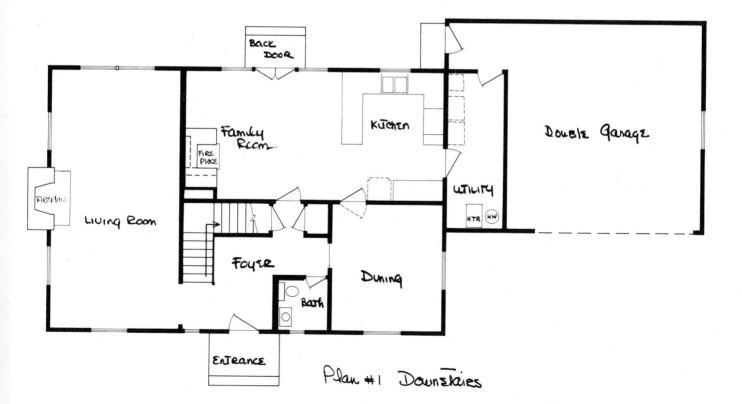

Plan #1 Downstairs

5

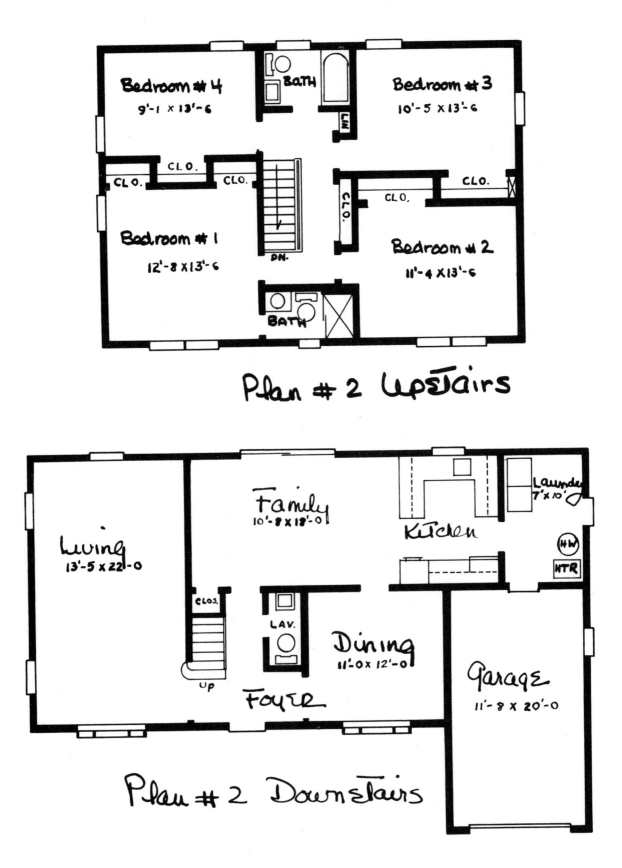

Bedroom # 4
9'-1 X 13'-6

BATH

LIN

Bedroom # 3
10'-5 X 13'-6

CLO.

CLO.

CLO.

CLO.

CLO.

CLO.

CLO.

Bedroom # 1
12'-8 X13'-6

DN.

CLO.

Bedroom # 2
11'-4 X13'-6

BATH

Plan # 2 Upstairs

Family
10'-8 X 18'-0

Laundry
7'x10'

Kitchen

HW
HTR

Living
13'-5 X 22-0

CLOS.

LAV.

Dining
11'-0 X 12'-0

UP

Garage
11'-8 X 20'-0

Foyer

Plan # 2 Downstairs

6

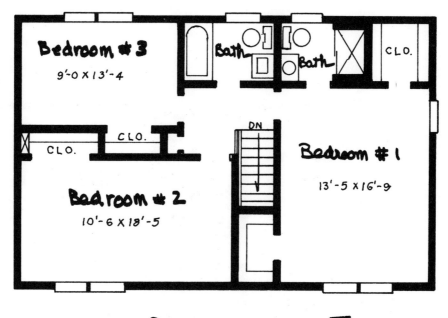

Bedroom # 3
9'-0 X 13'-4

Bath

Bath

CLO.

CLO.

CLO.

Bedroom # 2
10'-6 X 18'-5

DN

Bedroom # 1
13'-5 X 16'-9

Plan # 3 Upstairs

Laundry
7'-2 X 10'-8

HW

HTR

Kitchen
8'-6 X 10'-8

Family Room
10'-8 X 17'-9

Living
13'-4 X 22'-0

Dining
11'-0 X 12'-0

LAV.

11'-8 X 20'-0

Foyer

Plan # 3 Downstairs

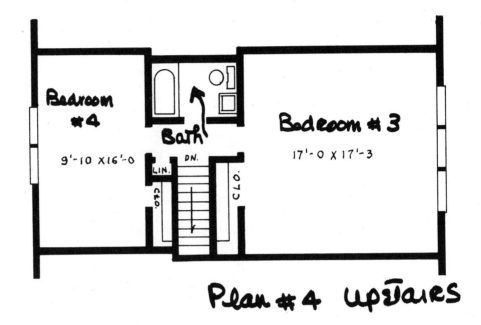

Bedroom #4

9'-10 X16'-0

Bath

Bedroom # 3

17'-0 X 17'-3

DN.

LIN.

CLO.

CLO.

Plan #4 Upstairs

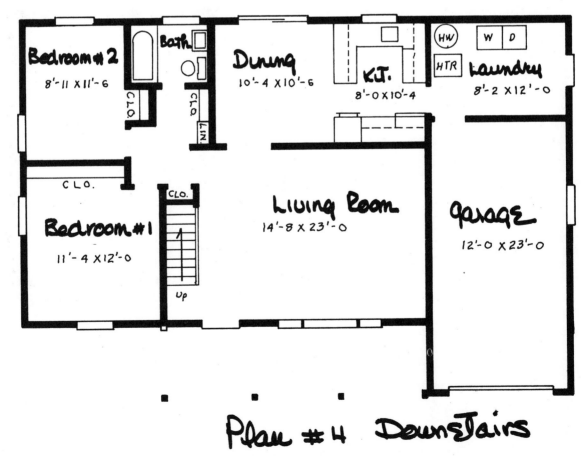

Bedroom #2

8'-11 X11'-6

Bath

Dining

10'-4 X10'-6

KiT.

8'-0 X10'-4

HW

W   D

HTR

Laundry

8'-2 X12'-0

CLO.

CLO.

LIN.

CLO.

CLO.

Living Room

14'-8 X 23'-0

garage

12'-0 X 23'-0

Bedroom #1

11'-4 X12'-0

Up

Plan #4 Downstairs

from 12 feet to 15 feet and even to 18 feet. Try for a house with a living room with the widest and longest dimensions. Of course, you can't select a home for living-room-size dimensions alone. The house must have other coordinating elements as well, such as an adequate and workable kitchen area.

3. In living rooms, look for cross ventilation and good sofa wall space. Plan #1 has good window expanse in the living room—a window at front and at back as well as a window at each side of the fireplace. Plan #2 has cross ventilation, as does Plan #3. Plan #4 has a window expanse at the front of the house only.

4. When selecting a two-story house, try, if possible, to find a house with a powder room/lavatory directly off the foyer, preferably with a window. Plan #1 suits the bill perfectly. Plans #2 and #3 both have powder rooms, but they are inside spaces without windows. Plan #4, an economy two-level home, has no powder room/lavatory, but it does have a bathroom located on the first floor close to the living room. This bathroom must service bedrooms one and two, as well as guests visiting the home for an evening. Those which have a dual-purpose bath off the living room and on the first level must utilize a decorating scheme within the bath that coordinates with the general parlor decor as well as with the decor in bedrooms one and two.

5. Dining rooms in development houses are generally, to my thinking, too small. They are adequate to seat four or six persons but rarely, if ever, large enough for a real family gathering of say ten or twelve. Some say I'm old-fashioned and that "for God's sake, Carleton, who entertains the old way anymore?" Nevertheless, I remain a firm believer in the family unit enjoying happy times together, and assuredly at a sit-down meal. Dining rooms measuring some 11 feet by 12 feet are just not large enough to accommodate more than five or six. If, perchance, you do have a home with a good-sized dining room, perhaps 12 feet by 15 feet, consider yourself in my category of the family-likes-company group. Inasmuch as I am forced by convention to utilize a dining-room space of 11 feet by 12 feet, I plan, under my section on "Dining Spaces," to present some ideas not only on the decorating but also on the functional use of the small dining area, or on "How to Serve a Family Gathering in Limited Space." I leave you with these words: as large a dining room as you can find, please!

6. A family room with kitchen seems to be standard in single-family houses being built today. Apparently we're getting old-fashioned again! Kitchens today are getting larger. Remember days gone by when the coal stove with poker sat in the end of the great kitchen? I remember them. I remember, too, the kitchen table where the family generally ate all meals and played cards on Saturday night. I even remember using the kitchen table for games and jigsaw puzzles. Somehow, during the late 1940s, with the development of more compact kitchen equipment, cabinets, and built-in eating counters, kitchens became more compact and less spacious. Everyone seemed to think

that eating on a counter was more fun than eating at the old kitchen table. Standing ovens were replaced by more compact stand-up units, and in the 1950s the ovens were even popped into wall-built cabinet units. The kitchens of the 1940s and 1950s were row-shaped—cabinets on one side, utilities on the other, and an aisle down the middle. People came to use the dining room more for evening meals and the kitchen counter for breakfast and lunch. Everyone thought it quite exciting to have one's own cafeteria or counter luncheonette right in the home. My parents followed the trend at the time, and my sister and I, too, thought the streamlined kitchen was great. Today, however, the swing is back to the kitchen as a general gathering place—and I'm delighted. The streamlined kitchen cabinets, utilities, wall ovens, and even electronic ranges are in their respective kitchen spaces, but those spaces are now larger. There seems now to be room for the sit-down counter as well as for the kitchen table. In some family kitchens there is room for a sofa, a coffee table, a family rocker, a club chair, a desk, and even a wall for a fireplace, television and built-in bookshelves. The family kitchen is today, indeed, the center of family activity.

7. The utility room is the boon of the working mother. By working mother I mean—what mother does not? If you're a mother taking care of an army or, seemingly, a tribe of little Indians, your work goes into the utility room. It is in this room that you have your washer and dryer. It is in this room that the family and the neighbors' children hang their winter coats, store their sleds, and take off their boots. The utility room in development, single-family houses generally adjoins the kitchen. The room should have a door to the outside as well as a door into the garage. Plans #1, #2, #3, and #4 are all perfect in their planning. Dad can come home at night, park the car, and enter the house without ever having to go outside. The kids can enter the house through the utility room door. The utility room door is, in fact, what we all used to call the "back door"! When selecting or buying a development house, make certain your utility room has a practical vinyl or asphalt-tile floor covering, as well as two doors—one to the garage and one to the outside.

8. Never let it be said that a growing family will ever have enough closet space. Sometimes, development houses today are built without cellar areas. Closet areas, therefore, must be large. Look for good closet space within the development house. Plan #1 has good closet and dressing space in the master bedroom area. Bedroom two in Plan #1 has two

closets with bifolding doors. Bedrooms three and four in Plan #1 each has one closet. Fortunately, in Plan #1 there is a cellar area, the door to the basement being located off the foyer, directly across from the guest closet.

Plans #2, #3, and #4 are houses built on what is called a "slab"; therefore, there are no basements in these plans. Closet space in the Plan #2 house is located on the first floor, directly behind the stair-case up. Closet space is also located as follows: two closets in bedroom one, one closet in bedroom two, one closet in bedroom three, one closet in bedroom four, one closet in the upstairs hall, and one linen closet. Let the buyer be the judge. If Plan #2 has enough closet space for his living needs, he will buy the house, provided everything else is to his liking. I frankly feel that Plans #2, #3, and #4 are lacking in closet space for the average growing single-family unit. Additional closet space will most likely be required, and this closet space will have to be built into the utility or laundry room, or perhaps into the bedroom area, if space permits.

9. Science and engineering have shown us that the heating system can be a small unit located in the utility room. The heating unit generally is complete with air conditioning as well. In Plans #1, #2, #3, and #4, you will note that there is a heating unit in each utility room as well as a hot-water heater. "HTR" stands for "heater" and "HW" stands for "hot water."

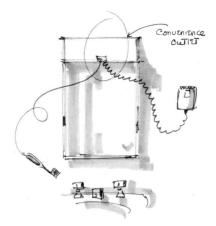

Convenience outlet

When buying a development house, be certain you understand the heating and air-conditioning complexities of the model you choose. Make certain, further, that you know what type of storm-sash windows will be supplied. Know if your triple-track storm sash includes sliding-track screens for all sliding doors. Screens are essential in summer as are storm windows and doors in winter.

10. Last, but not least important, an element to look for in the new community development house (or nondevelopment house, for that matter) you contemplate buying is the electrical outlet system. Make certain there are enough wall outlets in the living room. You will want to plug in the lamps on your end tables, and the plugs must go into a wall socket. Make certain there are wall plugs in the dining and kitchen areas, not only to accommodate lamps, but also as a convenience when using your vacuum cleaner. Be certain that the bathroom vanity mirror has a convenient outlet. Look for sufficient convenient electrical outlets in the kitchen, particularly above the counter top, for plugging in your electric mixer, rotisserie, electric frypan, toaster, blender, etc. Look for an electrical outlet in the ceiling over the place where your dining table will stand. You may want to hang a chandelier. Look for an overhead outlet in the foyer and in the upstairs hallway. In general, make certain your home has enough electrical wall and overhead outlets to suit your living needs.

The Room-To-Grow House (House Plans #5-#7)

Young couples who buy or build with expansion in mind are wise indeed. Expansion does not necessarily mean additions to the family. It might mean structural additions to the house. We show three models, Plans #5, #6, and #7. Plan #5 is in actuality a one-level house with room to grow in downstairs. It shows a small entry foyer with a six-step staircase up and a six-step staircase down. From the foyer rising up six steps, one finds a living room/dining room combination plan. The living room/dining room unit is most popular today and affords a young couple the opportunity to utilize one room for buffet entertaining as well as for family dining. There are many free-standing design and decorating ideas that can be employed in the layout planning of the living room/dining room combination. One especially attractive feature of this plan is the concrete patio. Eventually, the patio can be covered with flagstone, but for the time being it can be covered with an indoor/outdoor carpet. On a summer evening, a young

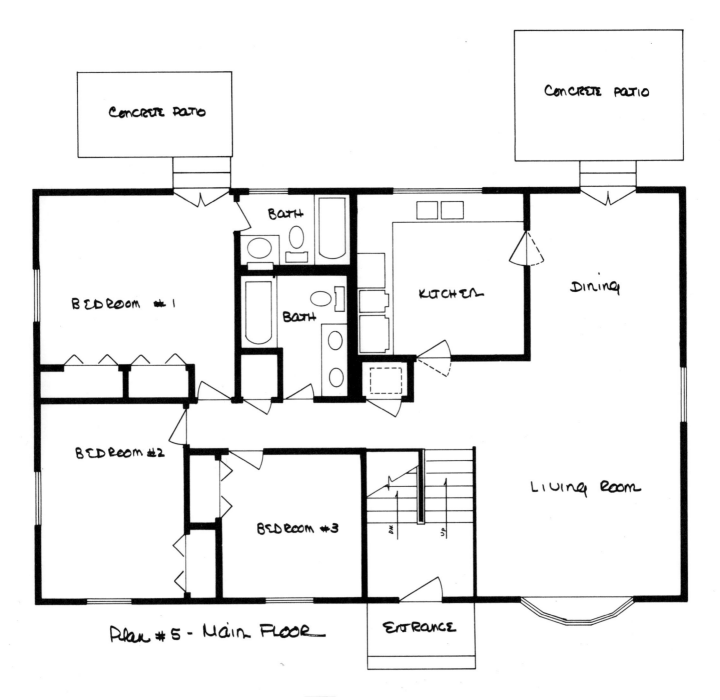

family can entertain by the barbeque cookout method on the patio outside the dining area. A long sweep of space is therefore created from the patio to the living room bay window. The plan also provides a patio outside the master bedroom. The master bedroom is most adequate in its planning of bath and closet space, there being two large closets in the bedroom area, as well as a separate and private master bathroom complete with tub and shower. In this plan, bedrooms two and three share the bathroom off the hall, and please note that two basins have been installed in the vanity lavette unit, which is good planning where space permits.

In essence, what one looks for in a split-level or in a one-story ranch house are the same elements as presented for houses under Plans #1 through #4, namely, adequate space and facilities to accommodate one's needs at the right buying figure.

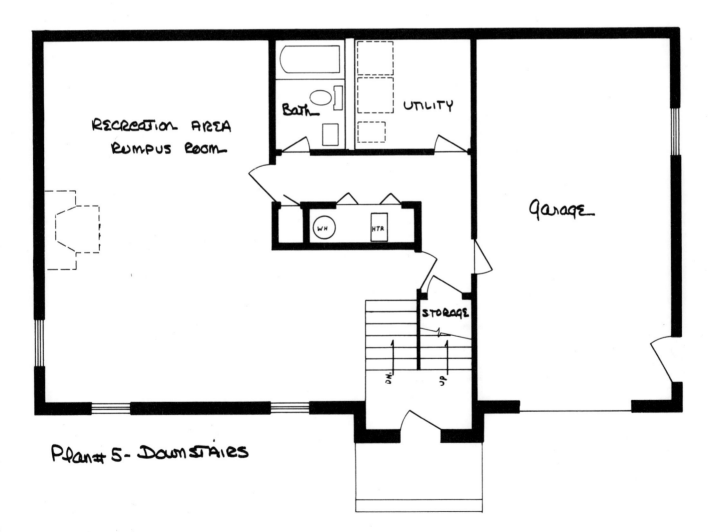

Plan # 5 - Downstaires

The lower basement area in Plan #5 is indeed large. The space in the drawing has been set up for a recreation room, complete with its own bathroom area. If one were contemplating buying a development house similar to that of Plan #5, the lower area would be left unfinished if funds did not initially permit the family to panel walls, install a fireplace mantel, tile or carpet the floor, install an acoustical ceiling, hang light fixtures, etc. When purchasing the house shown in Plan #5, the buyer would have the upper level completed. What would exist on the lower level would be the garage, which, when you study the plan, you will understand is located under the living room/dining room space. The utility room would be completed, as would the heating and hot-water closet room. The bathroom would be left unfinished, but the plumbing lines would be in place, wait-

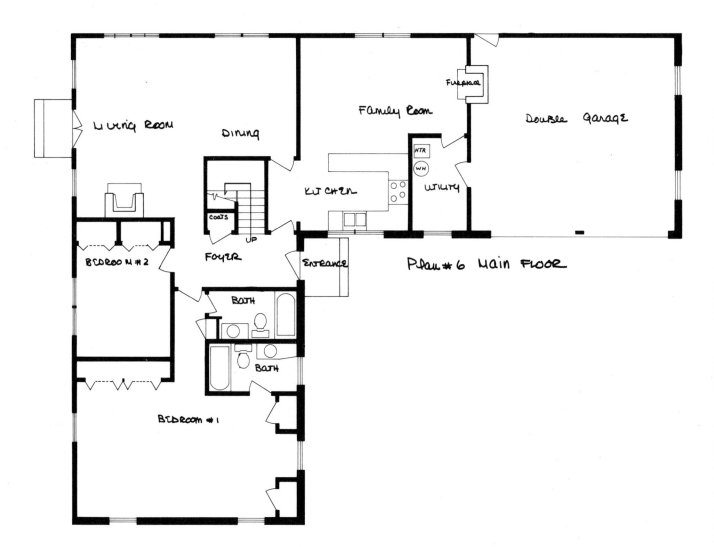

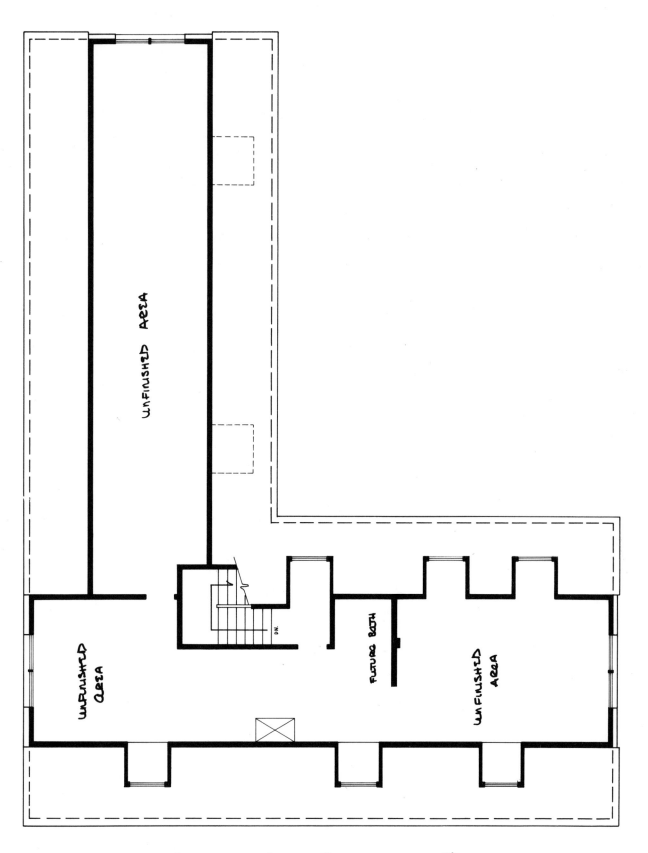

UNFINISHED AREA

UNFINISHED AREA

DN.

FUTURE BATH

UNFINISHED AREA

PLAN # 6   UPPER FLOOR - UNFINISHED
FOR FUTURE EXPANSION

ing for the day when the family has sufficient funds to buy bathroom fittings, tile, and vanity units. The door to the lower bathroom area would be installed, as would the necessary flues, etc., for the eventual fireplace. In a development house, all this can be easily accomplished and is done so more often than not.

Plan #6 is a house with room to grow in—not downstairs, but upstairs. This plan is for the family with one child but with thoughts of future family growth. The plan is not one with a basement area. All heating and hot-water equipment is located within the utility room. The plan is similar to Plan #5 in that both houses have combination living room/dining room setups. Plan #6 is similar to Plan #5 in that off the living room there is a concrete patio with French doors from the parlor to the patio. When one examines the upstairs plan, which is free of dividers (wall partitions), one can see that there is enough room for additional bedrooms upstairs, complete with baths. The young couple investing in a development house similar to that in Plan #6 would be wise to forget about finishing the upstairs area until necessary and concentrate on decorating and furnishing the downstairs area only.

Of particular note with respect to Plan #6 is the very ample-sized master bedroom, with four closet areas and separate, private master bathroom. The master bedroom is strategically closed off from the rest of the house by a doorway, providing Dad and Mom with blissful quiet. Young son, however, is within easy hearing distance. Bedroom two is an adequate-sized child's room or guest room directly across the hall from the second bath. The second bathroom in this plan must serve as the powder room/ guest bath also.

Plan #7 is a four-bedroom development house with great room for expansion in the basement area. The plan presented would be considered an eight-room house—living room, dining room, family room, kitchen-with-breakfast room, and four bedrooms. The plan shows extremely good foyer space, connecting bedroom space, and closet space. Note that bedrooms one, two and three all have walk-in closets. Bedroom four, or the guest bedroom, has its own private bathroom with a door from the bedroom side. Note also that there is a door from the guest bathroom to the hall area. This bathroom serves as a powder room when Mom and Dad are entertaining guests for an evening. Plan #7 offers great room to grow in. A house with four bedrooms usually means a family of at least six people, Mom and Dad with four children. In some cases, a four-bedroom house means five children. For such a family, one can be certain that a basement area is needed for the hobby, television, painting, erector set, doll-house room. The lower basement area usually also houses Dad's tool and fix-it shop.

When buying a development house in a new community, choose one with room to grow, not one that has just room to outgrow. Too often a young family buys with little thought about future needs and wishes. When buying a single-family home, do so with this practical question in mind: Does the house fulfill my projected future needs, as well as my immediate needs? Ask yourself secondly: Can I *afford* the home that fulfills the contemplated future needs of my family as well as my family's immediate needs? If you can answer both questions in the affirmative, you are on the right track.

If you find that you cannot afford the home that fulfills your contemplated future needs, examine your situation. Perhaps you would do best to rent a single-family house until such time as you can afford to buy a house. Or perhaps it would be best for you to reexamine your future needs. If your income does not warrant future family expansion, take this fact into account. Satisfy your immediate family needs and forget about family expansion for the present.

All on One Level (House Plans #8-#10)

The idea of the ranch house came to the East from the West. The California ranch house was rarely copied exactly. Eastern climates never were the same as desert or Southern California climates, and the ranch houses in the East were rarely made of the same materials as those in the West. But today, engineering science has worked out heating systems so that houses can be built around patios and indoor gardens, and one-level houses now are as popular in the East as they are in the West.

Plan #8 is a one-level house adequate for a family of five. The house has three bedrooms—one master with private bath, bedroom two for the two boys in the family, and bedroom three for the young sister. Note the location of the second bathroom in the plan, most conveniently spaced for guest use and equally conveniently located for the children. The hall linen closet is large enough for a family of five. The heating and hot-water mechanical system is located in its own closet area, off the entry foyer.

The family would find the family room in this model house most adequate. The dotted line dividing the kitchen from the family room indicates an overhead beam. The beam hangs over the center of a serv-

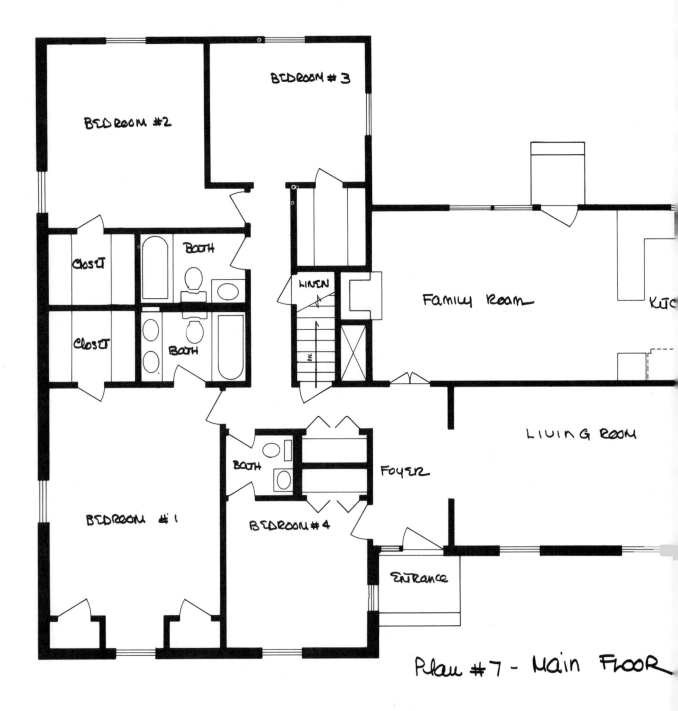

Plan #7 - Main Floor

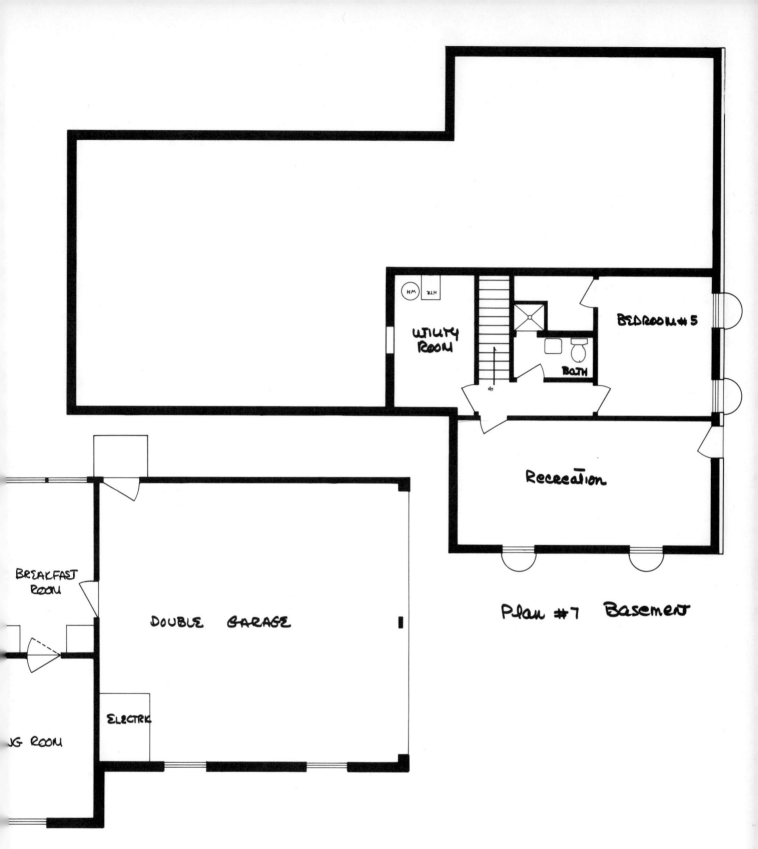

UTILITY
ROOM

HTR

WH

BEDROOM #5

BATH

Recreation

BREAKFAST
ROOM

DOUBLE GARAGE

ELECTRIC

G ROOM

Plan #7 Basement

21

ing sit-down counter. The back door in this house is actually directly off the family room. As in other plans shown, there is no direct outdoor access from the utility room. The utility room door does lead into the garage area, which is a help unpacking a car filled with groceries. There is room for adding a second-car garage to this house, as the dotted lines show. As in the other plans with living room/dining room combinations, this plan

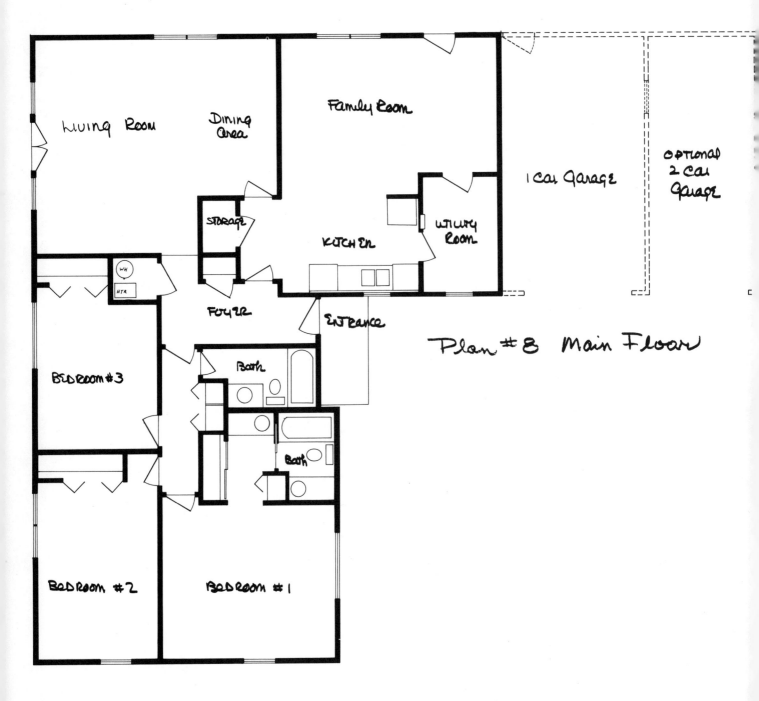

Plan #8 Main Floor

features a concrete patio outside the living room. I have always referred to the patio as being concrete strictly from a cost viewpoint. There is no objection to painted concrete, perhaps a grassy green or a color matching the living-room carpet. Of course, patios can be covered with flagstone or brick laid in the herringbone pattern or with black slate. But for the cost-conscious family, there is nothing whatsoever wrong with the painted-concrete look!

Plans #9 and #10 are basically the same. Each has a living room/dining room plan of the same dimensions; namely, the dining area is 9 feet by 11 feet, 9 inches, and the living room, 16 feet, 8 inches by 19 feet. The bedrooms are basically the same size, with two exceptions. Bedroom one in Plan #10 is one foot wider than bedroom one in Plan #9, and bedroom two in Plan #10 is an inch wider than its counterpart in Plan #9. The difference between Plans #9 and #10 is in the family room/kitchen space. Plan #10 shows a full family room with a breakfast alcove and kitchen. Plan #9 has only a family room/kitchen combination space. From a building-cost point of view, Plan #9 is, of course, more economical. Both plans have laundry/utility rooms with doors going out to and connecting with a one-car garage. Both

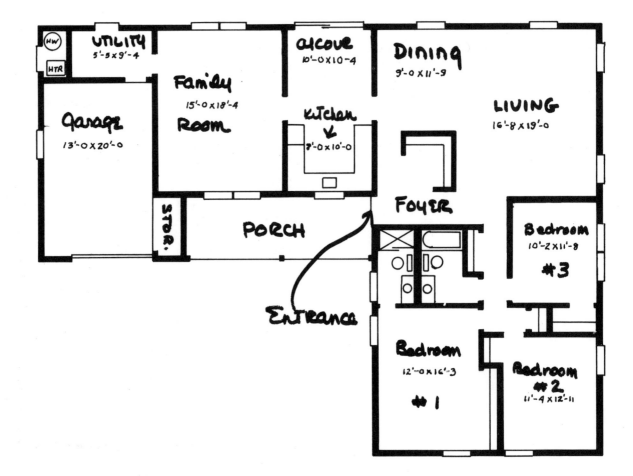

Plans #9 and #10 are built on a slab— that is, neither has a basement. Note, however, from an approach point of view, that both houses have what is known as a "porte-cochère," a French term meaning "door cover." The door covering in Plan #10 extends from the front door to the outdoor storage room, thus creating a small porch. While Plan #9 also has a porte-cochère, it is hardly long enough to create an exterior porch for much seating.

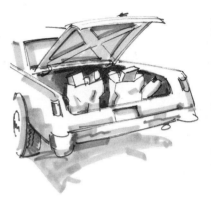

Decorating the Outside of Your Home

You know from my early comments on the two-story home that I am a great advocate of any color scheme which makes a home inviting from the outside. In planning model houses, I am always intrigued when it comes to the exterior coloring stage. Here are a few exterior color schemes for consideration:

House A

Basic color—Chocolate brown

Trim and shutters—White

Front door—Sky blue

House B

Basic color—Lemon

Trim and shutters—White

Front door—Royal blue

House C

Basic color—Pearl gray

Trim—White

Shutters—Deep gold

Front door—Deep gold

House D

Basic color—Williamsburg (pale green)

Trim—White

Shutters—Forest green

Front door—Forest green or white

House E

Basic color—Fawn beige

Trim—White

Shutters—Black

Front door—Black or cantaloupe

I like a white house with BLACK SHUTTERS
— and a Cherry-Cheery Red Door!

Try a color scheme of Pearl Grey - with white trim - deep gold shutters - and a deep gold front door

These five color combinations all presuppose light colors for basic tone, with generally white trim around window mullions and roof eaves. Window mullions are nothing more than dividing sections between glass window panels. I also like a strong contrasting color for shutters and doors. Matching the color of shutters and the front door is always effective. But try a different and exciting color for the door. In other words, the basic house color should be color #1, the trim color should be color #2, the shutter color should be color #3, and the front door color should be color #4. A word of advice—paint the front and back doors the same vibrant color.

On Doors and Decorations

The front door to any home should always say a friendly hello and welcome; try a special color for the door—perhaps cherry red, sunny lemon, sky blue, royal blue, or emerald green. Year round hang a cheery basket of seasonal flowers at the doorway above the knocker. The flowers can be

placed in pint bottles, the bottles being filled with wet floral styrofoam, which keeps the flowers fresh and in place as arranged. The styrofoam further prevents the water from spilling when the door is opened quickly.

For front door decoration, hang a pair of lanterns to the left and right of the door. These can be old English coach lanterns or brass hurricane lanterns or modern globe lanterns. For this you will need electrical outlets on each side of the door. Many homes, however, have only an outlet for a light fixture to be installed over the door, and in this case I suggest that a good-looking lantern bracket be installed. Local fixture stores, to say nothing of roadside antique shops, have a number of inexpensive light fixtures to choose from. You might find an old wrought-iron fixture or gas street light to re-make and install. Your front doorway needs light to be inviting and welcoming. Your front door should glow as does the window with the lighted lamp.

On Windows—Exterior Look and Design

Windows are the eyes of the house, and eyes should not be blinded. Windows should be graced with pretty curtains and draperies on the inside and perhaps with flower boxes and awnings on the outside. A window box serves as a polite shield from the eyes of passersby: a shield to ensure privacy within your own domain.

Novelty Decorations for Doors

When I was a boy growing up in the seacoast town of Nahant, Massachusetts, my mother and father, during the summer months when lobster-trapping season was in high gear, would hang a brightly painted lobster buoy, complete with cork rings, at the back door. There are many other novelty decorations for front and back doors, such as house names and eagles. Eagles hung over the doorway are most effective on Federal- and Colonial-type homes. Whatever decoration you choose, make it your own.

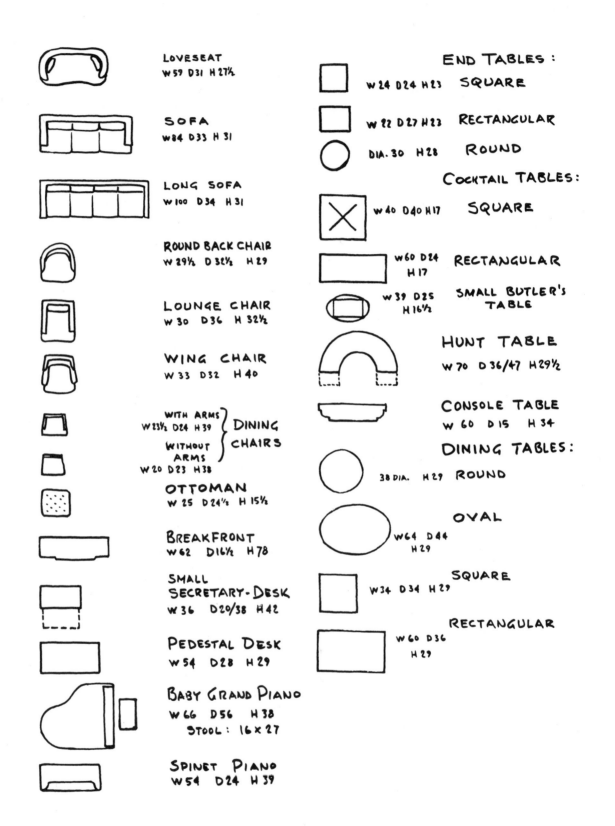

LOVESEAT
W 59 D 31 H 27½

SOFA
W 84 D 33 H 31

LONG SOFA
W 100 D 34 H 31

ROUND BACK CHAIR
W 29½ D 32½ H 29

LOUNGE CHAIR
W 30 D 36 H 32½

WING CHAIR
W 33 D 32 H 40

WITH ARMS
W 23½ D 24 H 39   } DINING
WITHOUT CHAIRS
ARMS
W 20 D 23 H 38

OTTOMAN
W 25 D 24½ H 15½

BREAKFRONT
W 62 D 16½ H 78

SMALL
SECRETARY-DESK
W 36 D 20/38 H 42

PEDESTAL DESK
W 54 D 28 H 29

BABY GRAND PIANO
W 66 D 56 H 38
STOOL: 16 × 27

SPINET PIANO
W 54 D 24 H 39

END TABLES:
W 24 D 24 H 23   SQUARE

W 22 D 27 H 23   RECTANGULAR

DIA. 30 H 28   ROUND

COCKTAIL TABLES:
W 40 D 40 H 17   SQUARE

W 60 D 24
H 17   RECTANGULAR

W 39 D 25
H 16½   SMALL BUTLER'S
TABLE

HUNT TABLE
W 70 D 36/47 H 29½

CONSOLE TABLE
W 60 D 15 H 34

DINING TABLES:

38 DIA. H 29   ROUND

OVAL
W 64 D 44
H 29

SQUARE
W 34 D 34 H 29

RECTANGULAR
W 60 D 36
H 29

32

Chapter II

Learning To Make a Furniture Layout of Your Home

Making a furniture layout is not so difficult as you might think. The starting point is to have on hand a layout or architectural plan of your home that shows room size, where ventilators are located, where doors are placed, where windows are located. In essence, the plan should show the fixed elements in your rooms, including the location of electrical overhead fixtures and electrical wall outlets. Those of you who live either in development houses or in homes that you yourself have built will have no trouble putting your hands on the original architectural house plans. Those of you who live in single-family houses that have not been recently built or that you did not build yourself will have to draw up your own house plan. Do not be upset! Follow these instructions and take your house measurements —room by room. Even if you do have plans, it is wise to check all the room dimensions to be certain the plans are correct. House plans are generally drawn on the $\frac{1}{8}$ scale or on the $\frac{1}{4}$ scale. The $\frac{1}{8}$ scale means that $\frac{1}{8}$ of an inch is equal to 1 foot; the $\frac{1}{4}$ scale means that $\frac{1}{4}$ of 1 inch is equal to 1 foot.

The first step I take in any development-house decorating project, or, for that matter, in any home-decorating project, is to measure all space, even if my client has complete architectural plans. And this is exactly what you should do! Take a folding rule or a long tape and start measuring room by room. Check the measurements noted on the plan and make the drawings accordingly. Know the length of the long wall in your living room. Check the width of the hall that connects and runs from your foyer to your bedrooms. Be certain that you know the size of your dining room. Know the size of all windows. Make certain that you indicate on your floor plan where columns or wall breaks occur in any of your rooms. All of these measurements are important as they will have a considerable effect on the layout of the rooms in your home. Above all, know where light fixture out-

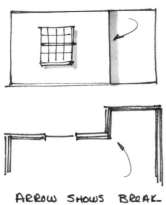

ARROW SHOWS BREAK
IN WALL

lets are placed and where wall electrical outlets have been installed. Many times, a sofa and end table layout in a living room has to be changed because there are no electrical plugs into which the end table lamps can be connected.

For those with floor plans or architectural blueprints drawn to scale, the checking of measurements with a tape measure or a folding rule is relatively easy. For those of you who have older single-family houses for which no blueprints or plans are available, there is no question about it. You will have to measure each room, and this process should begin before you start any decorating or place any furniture. It is best to draw a simple, even crude, floor plan of every room and then note dimensions. You can visually determine where one wall is longer than another and, when roughly drawing a room's floor plan, use your visual and common sense. If one wall in your living room is 22 feet long and the window wall is 14 feet across, you know that your 22-foot line on the paper must be longer than your 14-foot line. Even if the 14-foot wall looks longer on your drawing than the 22-foot line, get all the dimensions. With the use of a scale rule, you will be able to adjust the 22-foot and 14-foot walls so that they are in proper relationship to each other. When you have all the necessary measurements, you can then scale out your home accurately on paper. You don't have to be a draftsman or an architect or an interior designer to learn the simple art of scaling.

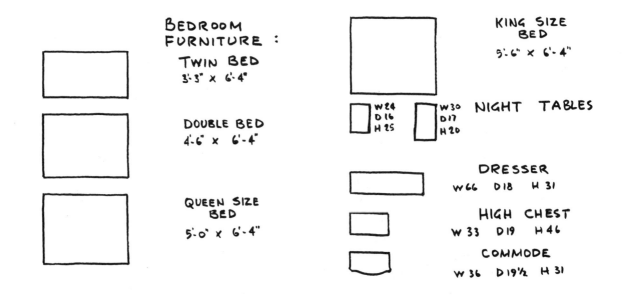

BEDROOM FURNITURE :

TWIN BED
3'-3" x 6'-4"

DOUBLE BED
4'-6" x 6'-4"

QUEEN SIZE
BED
5'-0" x 6'-4"

KING SIZE
BED
5'-6" x 6'-4"

W 24 D 16 H 25   W 30 D 17 H 20   NIGHT TABLES

DRESSER
W 66 D 18 H 31

HIGH CHEST
W 33 D 19 H 46

COMMODE
W 36 D 19½ H 31

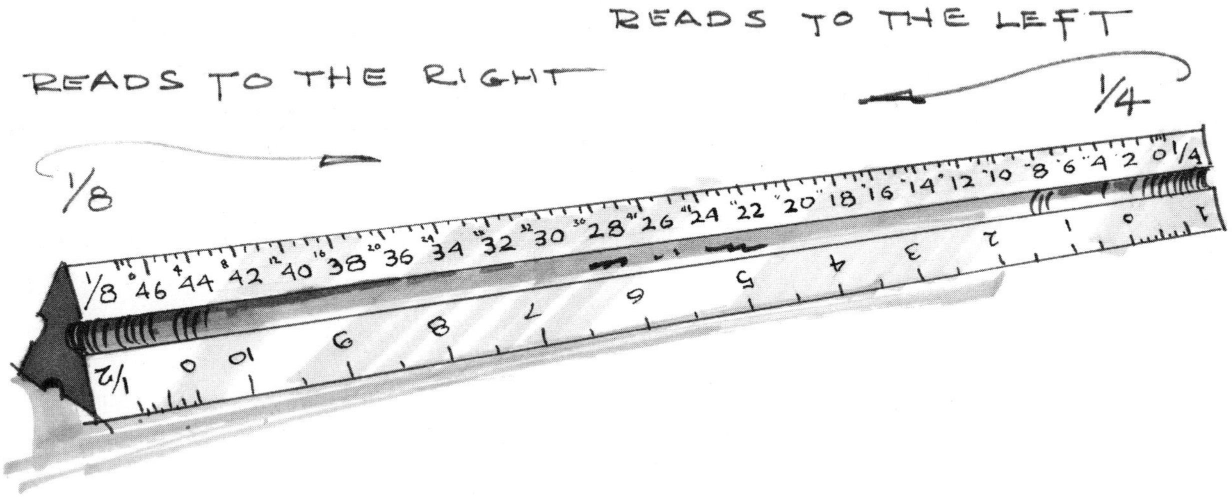
READS TO THE LEFT
READS TO THE RIGHT
1/4
1/8

The Scale Rule

The scale rule is one of the tools of the architect, draftsman, interior designer, and engineer. It is a ruler, much like the one you learned to read in the first grade. Whereas the school ruler is in inches, the scale ruler is divided into inches or parts of inches that represent feet. For example, pick up a scale rule such as the one shown in the illustration. At the far right side of the rule you will see the fraction ¼. This means that ¼ of an inch is equal to 1 foot. The space on the rule from the numeral 0 to the numeral 2, reading from right to left, is equal to 24 inches or 2 feet. The space on the rule from numeral 0 to numeral 46 represents 46 feet of space. The space on the rule from 0 to the first mark is equal to 6 inches. Each mark on the ¼-inch scale must be read from left to right. Each mark represents 6 inches.

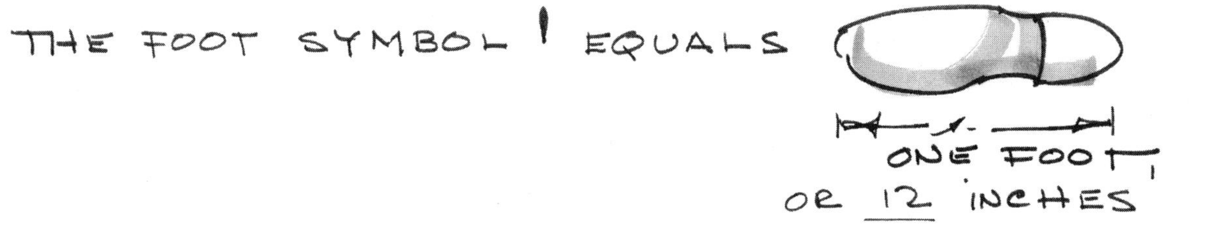
THE FOOT SYMBOL ' EQUALS
ONE FOOT,
OR 12 INCHES

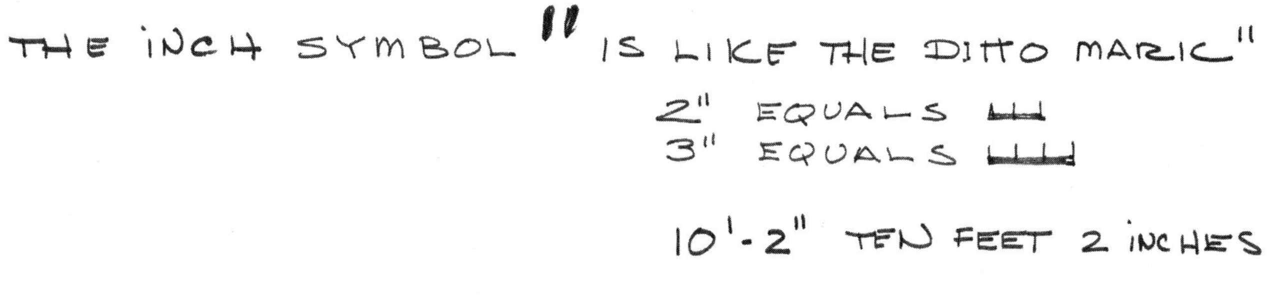
THE INCH SYMBOL " IS LIKE THE DITTO MARK"
2" EQUALS
3" EQUALS
10'-2" TEN FEET 2 INCHES

Thus, if you read with me the ¼ scale, you will be reading as follows: From 0 to the first mark = 6 inches; from 0 to the second mark = 12 inches or 1 foot; from 0 to the third mark = 18 inches or 1 foot, 6 inches and so on. The foot mark is represented by a simple line much like an apostrophe. The inch mark is represented by two marks much like ditto or quotation marks. Thus 2′2″ means two feet, two inches.

If you do not own a scale rule and you want to draw up an accurate plan of each room in your home, you can use an ordinary ruler, simply keeping in mind that each ¼ inch drawn on paper represents 1 foot of space. A 14-foot wall, for example, would be represented by a line 3½ inches long. To each inch there would be 4 feet on the ¼ scale, as inch ¼-inch mark on the ruler represents 1 foot.

For those who use the scale rule and who do not want to draw on the ¼ scale, you can use the ⅛ scale, the ½ scale, the ¾ scale, the 1 scale. Remember that the ¼ scale means that ¼ of every inch on the rule represents 1 foot. The ⅛ scale means that ⅛ of every inch on the rule represents 1 foot. The ½ scale means that ½ of every inch on the rule represents 1 foot. The 1 scale means that one inch on the rule represents 1 foot of space. The ⅛ on the scale ruler in the illustration reads as an ordinary ruler from left to right. From the 0 point to the first mark is 1 foot of space on the ⅛ scale. From the 0 mark to numeral 4 is 4 feet of space.

Generally, house plans are drawn on either the ¼ or the ⅛ scale. Very rarely, if ever, are house plans drawn on the ½-inch or 1-inch scale. However, people do find it easier to understand scale if a plan is drawn on the 1 scale. The 1-inch scale means that one inch of space drawn represents one foot. If you're one of those people who are not truly interested in the seeming complications of the ⅛ or ¼ scale, draw your house plans (by room) on the 1-inch scale. If you draw your rooms on the 1-inch scale, however, be prepared to use a large sheet of paper. One living room 14 feet wide by 22 feet long means that you must draw on a sheet of paper larger than 14 inches by 22 inches. If you're going to use the 1-inch scale and want all rooms on the same sheet of paper, start planning on a poster-size board. Whatever you decide scalewise, be certain your room plans are as accurate as possible. All wall breaks should be drawn, window areas indicated, and electrical outlets noted.

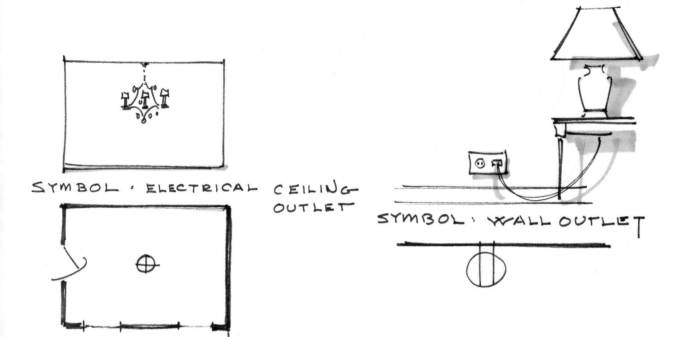

SYMBOL · ELECTRICAL CEILING OUTLET

SYMBOL · WALL OUTLET

Furniture Drawn to Scale

Many people who move into a new home do so without ever thinking of a furniture plan or a general layout. They simply move in and then decide where furniture should be placed and where pictures should be hung. Inevitably these people, after moving in, have to start juggling furniture. First they try the sofa and end tables just in front of the windows, then on the long living room wall. Then they try the sofa alone without the end tables. After determining, not assuredly, that the sofa belongs on the long wall with one end table, they wonder where to place the lounge chairs—perhaps in front of the window? Perhaps at the fireplace? Perhaps in the family room? I have known many people who try beds first on the bed wall with a night table between. Then they try splitting the twin beds and creating a studio-bed arrangement. These people are playing musical furniture. Everything is put in a line and then placed about until there is only one piece left. Unfortunately, the last piece in this game is not the winner, but neither is the big question piece of furniture that usually gets shoved into a corner or put away in the utility room next to the water heater.

Playing with furniture arrangement is a good idea, but it should be done in a layout plan prior to actually moving. In my design and decoration projects I know on arrival just where every piece of furniture fits into the layout at the moment it comes through the door. It is thus easy to direct the movers. When the sofa arrives, simply say, "Place the sofa on this wall," and so on. Whether you are in the throes of moving from a rented house to a house of your own or whether you are redecorating your living room, you should have a carefully thought-out plan as to where the furniture goes when it arrives. It would be foolish to buy a living room grouping of a 9-foot sofa, two end tables, two club chairs, one coffee table, a break-front, a round drum table, and two wing chairs, if your living room will accommodate only a 7-foot sofa, two small end tables, one club chair, one coffee table, one china breakfront and two side chairs. In order to avoid expense and the juggling-act approach to placing the furniture, plan a furniture layout for every room within your scaled drawings. Remember, furniture has sizes just as rooms do. Take your simple inch ruler or scale rule and draw the furniture in the plan. Try several ways of arranging the furniture until you come up with the room plan that is most comfortable for you. Many people actually do several furniture layouts before setting up a room or buying new furniture, because they want to be certain their own furniture or the furniture they are considering buying will fit within the space they have. These are wise people indeed.

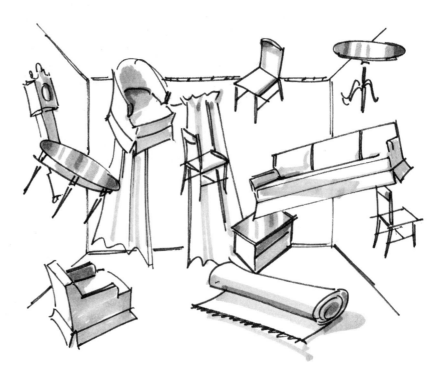

WILL YOU PLAY A JUGGLING ACT?

In order to lay out your rooms successfully, take an inventory of all your furnishings. This is known as an inventory list. On the list, the sizes of all furniture should be noted. For example, if your two end tables are 24 inches wide by 30 inches long by 19 inches high, these dimensions should be noted on the inventory. If your sofa is 8 feet long with three loose cushions and three loose backs, note on the inventory that the sofa is 96 inches long by $32\frac{1}{2}$ inches deep by $28\frac{1}{2}$ inches high.

PREPARE AN
INVENTORY LIST

Sofa arm heights are extremely important in the design picture as the height of the arm will affect the height of the end table or vice versa. A sofa with an arm height of $22\frac{1}{2}$ inches can accommodate an end table with a height of some 21 inches or 22 inches or 23 inches. Never use a 28-inch pair of end tables beside a sofa with an arm height of $22\frac{1}{2}$ inches. The tables are much too high. My general rule is that end tables can be some 2 inches lower or higher than the sofa arms. When the tables are 3 inches higher or lower, bad proportions result.

After, but only after, you have taken your inventory and you have noted the sizes of all your furniture, I recommend the juggling-furniture game, with paper furniture cutouts. Paper furniture cutouts can be made easily by anyone, particularly if he has been patient and learned to draw up a room to scale. There are, however, standard sizes of furniture which I have drawn to the $\frac{1}{4}$ scale and which will aid you in laying out the rooms in your home, if your layout is on the $\frac{1}{4}$ scale. Remember, if your layout is on the $\frac{1}{8}$ scale, your furniture cutouts must also be on the $\frac{1}{8}$ scale. If your rooms are scaled to the $\frac{1}{2}$ scale or the 1 scale, your furniture cutouts must be respectively on either the $\frac{1}{2}$ scale or on the 1 scale.

The Family Plans a Living Room Layout

The living room in the single-family house is a different thing to each and every member of the family. In planning the layout of a family living room, bear in mind that your end tables need not be matching: one table can be round or octagonal; the other can be square or rectangular, or it can be some interesting old three-drawer chest. If you do insist on matching end tables for your sofa with a rectangular coffee table, why not make the end tables round? A word of advice about coffee tables: Make sure that the table is lower than the seat of your sofa.

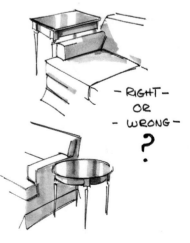

- RIGHT-
OR
- WRONG-
?

In the planning and layout of the living room in the illustration (it is the living room from house Plan #1), the sofa is on the long living room wall and it is flanked by a round, skirted end table and a group of nesting end tables. The skirted table is merely a piece of plywood with a wood column base, the table having been covered with a piece of round felt.

A friend of mine used an old stool for the base of her table. She got a round piece of ½ inch plywood, 30 inches across, for the top, nailed it to the bench seat and covered the whole with a felt cover. To determine the diameter of the felt table cover, measure the height of the table from the floor, multiply that figure by two and add the size of the plywood diameter. If you plan to use a felt-covered table next to your sofa, be certain your table height is approximately the height of your sofa arm. To do this, you may have to shorten the legs or reduce the height of the wood column if you use a pedestal base. For lounge chairs in the living room, I have used simple, skirted square-back chairs. The chairs are matching and pull up to a large coffee table. I like swivel-base lounge chairs in a grouping, such as that shown in the plan. The chairs can turn and face the fireplace as well as face the two wing chairs that are placed respectively to the left and right of the mantel.

TRY MAKING YOUR OWN COFFEE TABLE USING – A WIRE ROUND SPOOL – A TREE TRUNK – – A WAGON WHEEL – OR EVEN A BARRELL

One of my favorite pieces of furniture in the living room, or in any family room, library, den, or study, for that matter, is the coffee or cocktail table. I have seen some very interesting coffee tables come not from furniture manufacturers, but from the ingenious ideas of people. A friend of mine and his wife made a coffee table from an old round dining table simply by cutting down the legs! They painted the table with white lacquer and trimmed it in pale blue to match the wall color and general decorations in their living room. The table, being 42 inches in diameter, is large enough not to get crowded. A large coffee table is always preferable to small individual coffee tables. A group of nesting tables as shown in the floor plan can always be used when entertaining.

Another of my friends made a coffee table of the trunk of a large old tree that grew on his property and which eventually had to be cut down. The tree trunk was approximately 38 inches in diameter and was hollowed out from underneath to eliminate the weight problem in moving the piece about his living room. To reduce further the moving problem, my friend nailed six invisible roller casters onto the base. The top of the table, with its marvelous grain look, was given a natural stain.

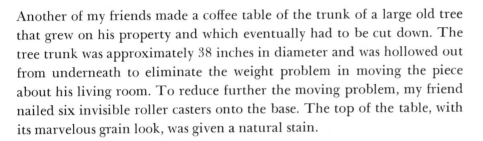

In the living room floor plan of house Plan #1, throw pillows have been tossed on the floor in front of the coffee table. The pillows for seating must be some 18 inches square. Two pillows should be used for each pillow seat, one on top of the other. The pillows on the floor at the coffee table make the sofa conversation grouping adequate to accommodate eight people. Additional seating is provided by the two wing chairs.

In planning seating arrangements, be sure each chair has a small occasional table at its side to hold an ashtray, and perhaps a lighter or a bowl of flowers or a magazine. I am not keen on chairs standing alone, nor do I like walking into a room and seeing the back of a sofa. Try in your planning to make certain your sofa guests as well as your lounge-chair, occasional-chair, or wing-chair guests have a place to rest whatever they care to rest. In the living room plan illustrated, the three sofa guests can use the cocktail table or the end tables. The pillow squatters can use the coffee table. The wing-chair guests can use the cigarette tables placed beside each chair. The desk chair is serviced by the desk, as is the desk pull-up chair.

When looking for cigarette tables to accommodate the wing-chair guests,

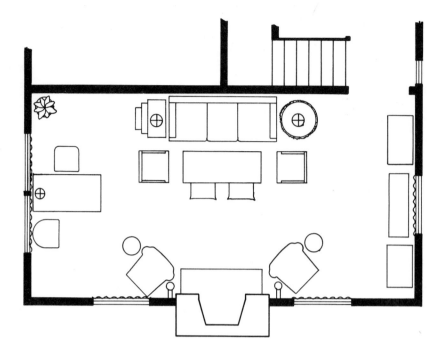

don't try for matching pieces, but rather for individual tables with some character. One of my friends uses a small table with a plate on top as a cigarette table next to one of her wing chairs and an old, interesting standing ashtray next to her other chair. Much can be done with old men's-club cigarette urns. Spray the bases a pretty color to go with your room's decor, and replace the old clear-glass ashtray with an interestingly designed saucer, preferably one which has lost its cup mate.

At the front window in the plan (to the left on entering the room), a bench is used. The bench can have a back or only an upholstered seat. On each side of the bench are commodes. The commodes do not have to match. In fact, one might be a high piece with glass shelves for ornaments, and the other can be a three-drawer piece over which is hung a mirror or a picture grouping. I love a room with balance, but balance can be achieved in many ways other than by matching pieces. Note in the illustration how balance has been achieved with the bench in front of the window and with the commode to the left and the vitrine to the right.

Lighting is discussed in a separate chapter, but for the moment note how well this particular room is lit. There are lamps on the end tables, on the desk, and on the commode. There is lighting within the vitrine cabinet, and there are two wall sconces to the left and right of the mantel. If your living room has no fireplace, you may wish to study the alternate layout which I have shown.

The Living Room/Dining Room Combination

The living room/dining room combination is seen more and more today in single-family American houses. Such an arrangement combines two rooms and makes for informality. In fact, many people prefer the living room/dining room arrangement over the separate living room and dining room setup. Such families generally feel that the separate living room becomes an unused, even unfriendly room. "I don't want my children ever to feel they cannot use a room in our home," one mother recently told me. I understand this mother's feelings, yet a separate living room need not necessarily be an unfriendly room. Children who grow up in single-family houses with combination living room/dining room areas must learn to regard that room with the same respect as the children who grow up in homes in which there is a separate living room and dining room. Children soon learn that enjoyment of a room does not mean destruction, provided their parents take pride in their home, in the furnishings they have acquired, and in their manner of living.

As a model for the living room/dining room layout we will use house Plan #8. The sofa and end tables have been placed along the far wall, the far wall in this case being the wall farthest from the entrance to the living room from the foyer. Again, as I have stated, the end tables do not have to match. One end table is a sewing basket/standing lamp unit; the

second one is a round table with four legs and a magazine shelf below. Pulled up to the sofa and to the coffee table are two chairs—not matching. One is a comfortable club chair with cushioned back and seat; the second is an interesting old rocker. The rocker seems to go hand in hand with the sewing basket/standing lamp end table. I'm partial to rockers in my own home and I have a bentwood rocker with cane back and seat. I find it the most comfortable chair in my apartment. Compare my rocker with the Kennedy rocker in the illustration. You don't have to have a Kennedy rocker in your home, nor do you have to have a rocking chair similar to my own. However, do consider the use of a rocker somewhere in your home, perhaps in your family room or in your den. It's possible to find an old-fashioned rocker for very little money, though you might have to refinish its frame or repaint it a bright color.

THE KENNEDY ROCKER

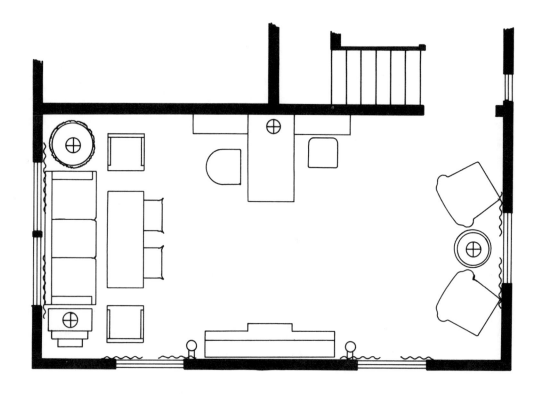

In the plan, the rocker has beside it a handy end table. The lounge chair has a round table at its right and a small muffin stand to the left. Notice that the floor space directly in front of the French doors that go to the patio has been left free. Leaving this area open is what is called in interior planning "creating a traffic pattern." Furniture should never be in the passage to an entrance or an exit.

On the wall to the left of the room's entrance from the foyer is a love seat or bench grouping, complete with a wall of built-in cabinet and book space. The grouping is illustrated in my sketch. Somehow or other, the minute I mention built-in units to my friends or clients, their eyelids flicker like the changing numbers on a cash register. Everyone thinks that built-in units are terribly costly. Not so. Oftentimes, they are not so costly as pieces of furniture, such as hutches and breakfronts. Nevertheless, built-in units scare people because they find them complicated. Generally, people like to know exactly what they're getting and they look upon built-ins as unknowns. They can't go to a local department store or to a furniture store and see their built-in before they buy it.

– MY ROCKER –

A built-in unit is not a complicated thing nor should it be considered an unknown. Indeed, there is no reason that you can't design and plan your own unit. You don't have to be an artist or a draftsman to know what you want from a built-in bookcase/cabinet piece. You may want cabinets on the bottom and bookshelves on the top. Take your drawing, no matter how crude, to a local cabinet man or carpenter. Show him your sketch and

ask him what he would charge you to build and install your cabinet/bookcase. Make certain he builds the unit of kiln-dried wood—you don't want any warping! You can have him install the piece unfinished and you can be your own painter or stainer. You may want to paint the piece the same color as your walls, or you may want to paint it a color to sparkle your living room/dining room decor. You may even want to paint the piece white and line the back of the bookshelves with the same fabric that is on your living room sofa.

If you have some mechanical ability and know how to cut wood to size and assemble cabinet doors, construct your built-in unit yourself. All you have to know is the depth you wish your bookshelves, the height you wish your cabinets, the way to install doors with hinges, and the manner in which to install uprights to hold your bookshelves.

In the plan, I have shown love seats, fully upholstered. If you prefer a country look to your home, find some old wood benches to use as pull-ups to your built-in unit. The benches are often referred to as deacon's benches.

In the living room of their Colorado home some friends of mine used old church pews which they had picked up from a local church that was being demolished. They left the dark mahogany finish and made colorful and attractive pads for the seats. Other friends of mine have used old school benches as sofa seating groupings in their home. One can do great things in the home with old school benches, church pews, and rush-seat benches, as well as with deacon's benches. As pull-up chairs to the love seat or deacon's bench or church-pew grouping, find a pair of individual small chairs. Again, the pull-up chairs do not have to match. One might be a cock-fighter's chair and the other a chair with an upholstered seat and back. Pull-up chairs with arms are the most comfortable and welcoming. In the illustration you will see a cock-fighter's chair. It has no back—only a front!

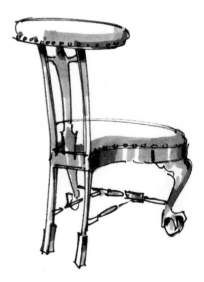

Our Plan #8 house has a direct service from the kitchen into the dining room. This is good planning and makes for ease and convenience. The table shown in the drawing is a standard oval table with four rush-seat ladder-back chairs. Two chairs are placed against the wall which can be pulled up to the table if necessary. The dining area in Plan #8 living room/dining room setup is for a family of six.

Many imaginative things can be done with dining rooms and with living room/dining room setups by following the country look. In a small summer home I once had on Long Island, I made my own dining table, using sawhorses and boards. You can see such a table in my drawing. I painted the two sawhorses a bright lacquer red and made the tabletop of planks, which I fitted together with industrial glue. As chairs, I used picnic-type pull-up benches on each long side. At the head of the table I used old rush-seat chairs that I found for six dollars in a roadside junkyard. The chair frames were painted red and the seats I left in the natural rush.

The distribution and planning of light in the living room/dining room shown in the plan is, as always in every home, of the utmost importance. Lighting must be evenly distributed in a room to make it comfortable and attractive as well as functional. Function, I believe, is the most important element in any room! Note that there is a lamp on the round magazine

end table next to the sofa. The sewing basket is a standing-lamp piece. There are two reading lamps that sit on the top of the built-in cabinet, directly under the bookcases. The dining room is lighted by a fixture that hangs over the dining table and by a pair of lighted wall brackets that are located above the chairs that sit against the wall.

Another Suggested Living Room/Dining Room Plan (House Plan #6)

In the general layout of house Plan #6, which has a fireplace, I have put up two dividers between the dining room and the living room. Note that the divider panels are not closing. The great advantage of a living room/dining room combination is its spaciousness. To close up this spaciousness is to make a serious mistake.

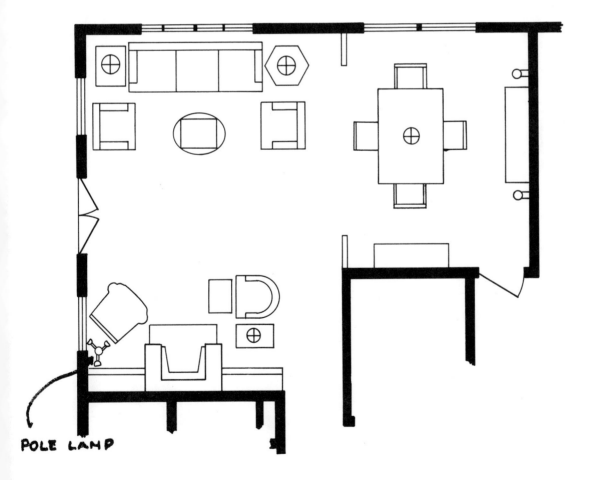

POLE LAMP

The divider panels between the living room/dining room shown here can be one of a number of things. They can be louvers, filigree screen panels, or trellis panels. They can be solid panels painted an attractive color or plywood panels covered with fabric. They can be striped panels or panels covered with wallpaper or contact paper. They can be stained wood panels with hanging pots of ivy. They can be spindle panels or simple old posts. All these treatments are illustrated in the hope they will provide a few ideas on how to divide your living room/dining room spaces economically and with the least amount of effort. Space dividers between living and dining areas in the single-family home should carry only a suggestion of division —a suggestion only. Many people use plants, either hanging or standing, to suggest this division.

50

The Family Room (House Plan #7)

The family room is not the destructible room. It is the indestructible room of the home, where the walls are covered with washable vinyl or with a wood laminate or 1/4-inch plywood. It is the room with the vinyl or vinyl-asbestos tile floor. It is the room where all upholstery on chairs as well as sofa is of naugahyde. It is the room with dustable and washable louver shutters. In essence, the family room in the single-family home is a room that must be planned, decorated, and furnished in the most practical, indestructible way.

I recall a mother telling me recently when I was designing and decorating her playroom, "Remember, Carleton, no fabrics; nothing that cannot take wear. My three boys will be riding their bicycles in this room." One must always take into consideration the function and use of a room when planning its design, decoration, and furnishing.

In the family room of model house Plan #7, a white and black vinyl floor was installed throughout the entire area, including family room, kitchen and breakfast room. The flooring was of an overall pattern, specks of black on white, for practicality. (A solid-white vinyl floor or a solid-black vinyl floor shows every scuff or soil mark.) The walls were covered with a white, birchlike laminated plastic. The bookcases to the left and right of the fireplace were of white birch painted with a washable lime-green semigloss enamel. Kitchen cabinets had white birch laminated fronts, and the counter tops were of a red-linen plastic laminate. Window louver shutters were painted with a lime-colored lacquer to match the built-in bookcases. All ceilings were covered with contact paper, the design being bright red cherries with green leaves on a white background. Upholstered furniture was all covered with vinyl—the sofa in red naugahyde, the lounge chair at the sofa grouping in black naugahyde, and the seats of the two white-lacquered rockers beside the television set also in red naugahyde. Accent pillows for the sofa

were of lime-green and white naugahyde. I draw particular note to the color scheme for this family room as the coloring was crisp and bright. Many people mistakenly feel that the only practical colors are dark beige, brown, and cocoa combinations. Nothing could be further from the truth. Today you can create a practical and washable interior of the crispest snowy whites, soft lemon yellows, powder blues, petal pinks and springtime greens. Don't be afraid to decorate your family room with bright, gay colors. Just be certain that the materials you use are practical, washable, and easily maintained. Many people feel that louver shutters are costly for family room decor. There is no question about it. Louver shutters, particularly in a special color finish, are more costly than draw draperies or window shades. If you want to reduce expenses in the decoration of your family room, try installing draw draperies of a colorful, washable fiber glass. You might even try curtains of a washable polished cotton or inexpensive duck cloth. If you're handy with a stencil, you might even install simple, white opaque shades on your family room windows. Stencil a large cherry motif or some other design on the shade to coordinate it with the overall room decoration. The illustration shows several window-treatment ideas for family room windows that are both practical and inexpensive.

The bottom café curtain with the ruffled top can give your family room windows an interesting and attractive look. The back curtains of white, washable duck cloth, trimmed with a border of bright fabric, can also give your family room windows an exciting look. Even upper and lower café curtains made of unlined felt can add gaiety.

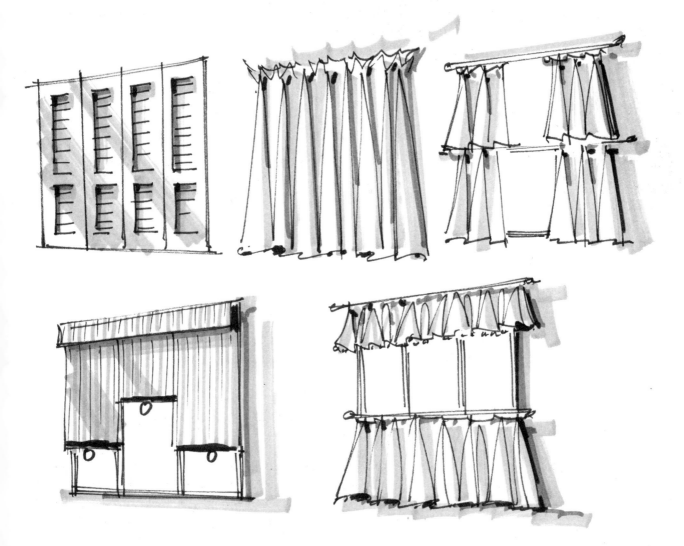

If a plastic laminate for the walls in your family room is not within your current budget, use a solid-color contact paper.

The Master Bedroom—A Haven for Mom and Dad (House Plan #3)

In every single-family home there is always a bedroom that is larger than the other bedrooms. This room has an unwritten sign on the door that says "Reserved for Mom and Dad." In the layout of the master bedroom of house Plan #3, the double bed is on the facing wall. Beds should always be placed on the wall farthest from the entrance door. To the left and right of the bed are night tables, each with a lamp. I am as much against matching night tables as I am against what is commonly called the "bedroom suite." Balance and color coordination are essential, but this does not mean everything has to match. One night table may be a chest table, or a round skirted table or a table without a drawer or with a drawer, or it may be a cabinet. The other could be an old restained trunk, or an old bachelor's chest, or it might be one of those old telephone-table desks repainted and fixed up with new hardware. The legs of the telephone-table desk will have

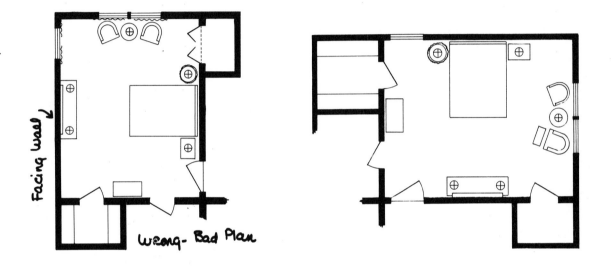

Facing wall

Wrong- Bad Plan

to be cut down to the proper night-table height—somewhere between 20 inches and 25 inches. In the bedroom shown in the plan, there is a standard high chest for Dad and a long dresser chest for Mother. The high chest and long dresser are standard and basic pieces of furniture for the master bedroom. If you are a bedroom-suite buyer, you can find the entire set—low chest, high chest, night tables, and headboard—to match. (Footboards seem to be out of vogue these days in the bedroom-suite category, but don't count on that. Three weeks after you read these pages, footboards may be in again.)

Be your own judge as to whether you prefer the matching bedroom-suite plan or the harmoniously uncoordinated furnishing plan for the bedroom. The two sketches show the difference!

Granted, the non-suite plan takes more time to bring together; but it offers much for satisfaction.

On Beds and Headboards

Whatever the layout of the master bedroom, twin beds or a double bed, there are from a decorating viewpoint a host of different types of beds and headboards. A young couple who live in a single-family home on Long Island have the most beautiful brass double bed with a headboard and footboard I have ever seen. As night tables, they found two old chests,

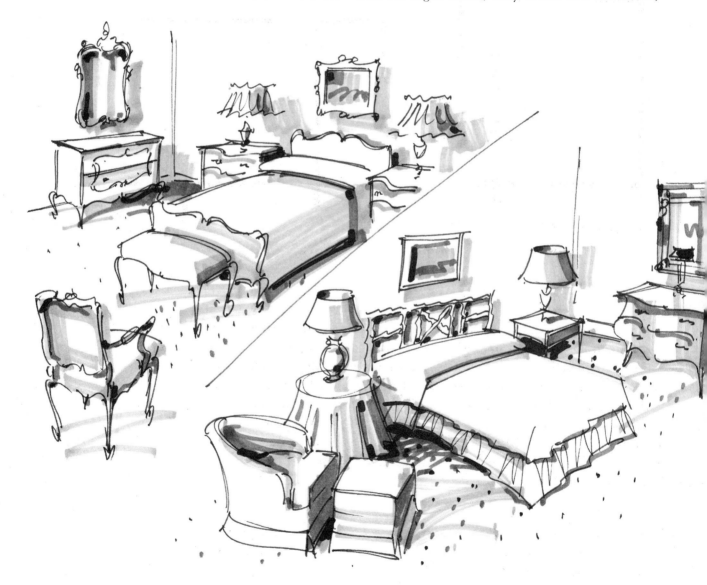

which they painted white and slightly antiqued with umber. The chests were later trimmed with a soft green paint. Their dresser chest is an old country piece which they painted soft green. They changed the hardware, replacing the old pulls with shiny brass 2-inch doorknobs. The chest coordinates beautifully with the brass bed and white antique night tables. In their honor and in tribute to their creativity, I have shown Bill and Kathy's bedroom in my illustration.

Unlike my young friends, you may not be a brass-bed enthusiast. If you prefer an upholstered headboard, make certain you use practical washable

fabric. Have you ever seen the look of an upholstered headboard that has had two oftentimes greasy heads as its bed companions? Whenever my clients ask for upholstered headboards, I always suggest a fabric that has been treated with one of the many stain repellents. Upholstering the headboard

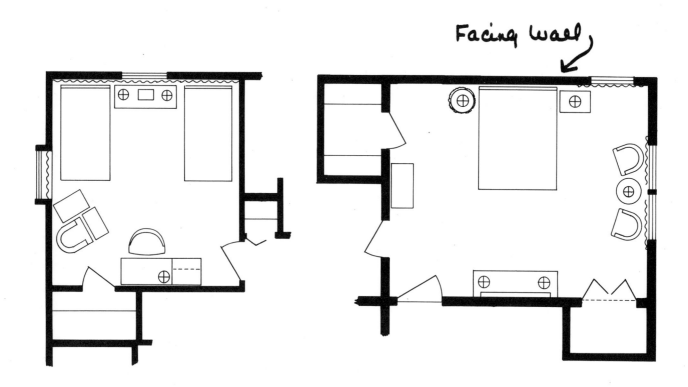

Facing wall,

in vinyl is the most practical approach. On occasion when I suggest the vinyl-covered headboard, the young wife will look at me with an air of indignation. "How can you suggest covering a headboard in such a commercial, hotel-looking material?" Granted, many hotel and motel headboards are covered with vinyl, for practicality. Most often the vinyl materials used are coarse and inexpensive. However, there are a number of vinyls on the market now that look and even feel like fabric. There are also vinyl upholstery materials with a glovelike softness. There are a number of other approaches to take when considering a headboard. Why not try the bolster effect with a wood rod? The bolsters are attached to the pole either by fabric loops or by wood or brass rings. The wood- or brass-ring attachment follows the same principle used in the hanging of café curtains. For another headboard suggestion, there is the fabric panel. The wall behind the bed is covered with a fabric covering, preferably the same as that used on the bedspread; the fabric panel goes on the wall, from baseboard to ceiling. For more traditional tastes, the testa canopy bed is a possibility. This can be purchased in the furniture department of most leading department stores. If you're a bug on buys, you might find an old testa headboard and footboard frame in one of the many wayside antique shops around the country. In addition, there are headboards made of stainless steel; there are cane headboards, bamboo headboards, fretwork headboards. You can even use as a headboard an interesting old carved door.

Comfort in the Master Bedroom

The master bedroom should have a seating area, preferably two lounge chairs and one ottoman grouped about a round occasional table with a lamp. Such a grouping provides a place and means for weary parents to relax in the privacy of their own room. Sometimes bedroom areas are small and two lounge chairs might be an impossibility. In that event, one chair, preferably with ottoman, should be used.

A Room for the Little Girl (House Plan #1, Bedroom Three)

Decorating a little girl's room is a delight because the furnishings available are so fanciful and of such a wide variety and assortment. A few months back, I was talking about color with an editor of one of our top magazines, and how one determines his or her own favorite color or color schemes. Allison's reply to me was most fascinating. She said, "Carleton, why don't you assemble a group of colored paintings or prints? When you are talking with a client about color and the selection of color for any given room, toss the pictures or prints on the table and ask for an immediate like or dislike reaction. Put the positive likes in one pile and in another pile the dislikes." By looking through the likes, I would observe a trend in color preference, be it reds and blues as predominant colors in the positive pile, or yellows and greens as the predominant colors in the negative pile. I have tried this color-preference test with my adult clients and have used it as a game with small children. The paintings and prints I use in my color game with children are ones they can relate to. A Raggedy Ann print with lots of reds and blues would be shown along with a seashore scene of yellows, oranges, and pale blues. I never use only prints or pictures of identifiable children's favorites, for the child might pick the Raggedy Ann over Humpty Dumpty solely because she likes Raggedy Ann better than Humpty Dumpty. As a result of this game I can definitely state that strawberry pink, pale pink, and white are the favorite colors of little girls. I had to determine the validity of the theories "Pink for little-girl babies" and "Blue for little-boy babies" in my own way. The theory certainly works for girls. Boys and blue are something else again!

When planning a room for a little girl, stick to the powder-pink, white, and strawberry color plan. Be certain to use only strawberry pink. In my picture-testing game, I have found that little girls shy away from bright reds. The strawberry color must be strawberry.

Even if you have only one daughter, make certain you plan the room with twin beds. Girls love to have sleep-over company. A little girl's room should have a dresser, and in my plan I have placed it between the beds, complete with two lamps. There should be a desk to double as a dressing table, if necessary. To the left of the desk on the plan is a 36-inch chest of drawers on top of which, indicated by dotted lines, is a bookcase hutch to be used for doll collections. The necessary bulletin board can be constructed with cork board covered with some pale pink or strawberry felt, the whole surrounded by a white frame. Or instead of a wood frame, glue grosgrain strawberry-colored ribbon around the perimeter. The bulletin board can be hung on the wall with an invisible back wire or suspended on a strawberry-colored grosgrain ribbon hanger, as indicated in the illustration.

Every bedroom in the home should have a comfortable chair. In the plan, I have placed a chair-ottoman next to a wicker storage basket. I have found wicker works well for headboards and accessories in a little girl's room. There are natural-finish wicker headboards in a wide variety of designs, as well as wicker toy baskets, night tables, and chairs. These can be sprayed any color you like. If your daughter follows my color test, spray her wicker headboards a spanking clean white and trim them in strawberry pink. You might likewise paint her toy chest the same colors, white with a strawberry trim. There are a number of lines of children's furniture on the market and you can take Sis to a local furniture store to pick out her own pieces. Visit the local lumber shop or hardware store that sells unpainted furniture. There you can buy a dresser chest and a desk unit that you can spray-paint with a soft pink lacquer. The hardware on unpainted furniture is usually white porcelain, which is most effective with white wicker pieces. Line the drawers of the dresser and desk and 36-inch chest with a pink and white striped contact paper. Use the same pink and white paper to line the back part of the bookcase, as well as the walls in Sis's closet.

For further general hints on the decor, see the illustration.

A Jungle for Junior (House Plan #8, Bedroom Three)

Boys, unlike girls, never pick pink and strawberry as favorite colors. When I play my picture color game with young boys, the results are somewhat surprising. Favorite colors of boys between the ages of six and twelve seem to be bright reds, chocolates, cocoa browns, oranges, and yellows. Blue, for some reason, is almost never chosen. Greens also seem to play a secondary role. While girls seem to prefer solid-color fabrics over figured patterns, boys always seem to pick out printed materials. I have also found that young boys like all the animal fabrics. When a zebra, pony, leopard, or tiger fabric or a plaid or large-checkered fabric is shown to a boy, his eyes light up. If you give your son's room a touch of the jungle in your decor planning, you are giving the little tiger exactly what he wants. You're also safe with plaid carpets or fabrics.

Somehow or other, when it comes to getting the second-largest bedroom in a house, it always goes to the girl. I can remember when I was a young boy and my sister and I were bickering for a certain room in the house, the second-largest bedroom, mind you, my dad would say, "Let Vivian have the room, Carl! Remember, she's the girl!" I never did understand Dad's reasoning, but she always got the second-largest bedroom and yours truly ended up with the smallest. It always seems to work out that way even today. So, to all boys with sisters, grumble not and face the reality that Sis does have more clothes than you have! She does need more closet space than you do and she does stay in her room and use it more than you do yours.

In the layout plan shown in the illustration, Junior's jungle is planned in the studio manner to give more floor space. The bed with bolsters can be a standard 3-foot 3-inch bed with a corduroy cover, or it can be a trundle bed. The illustration shows a trundle bed with one bed fitting under the other for use by sleep-over guests. A corner-desk arrangement is shown with two 36-inch-wide chests in the bedroom planning. Each 36-inch chest has a bookcase unit above to house toy cars, airplane glue, Yo-Yos, school books, baseball cards, amateur radio-operator's equipment, as well as baseball cap and glove.

For Junior's room, a bulletin board is also a definite must, and the plan shows the bulletin board hung on the wall over the trundle bed. Junior's chair should be covered in a practical upholstery material, perhaps a bright red, yellow, or chocolate-brown naugahyde, depending on whether you go to the jungle or to the Scottish highlands in your decor planning for the room. If jungle is your preference, cover the club chair in one of the fur-designed naugahydes. There are imitation-pony naugahydes as well as imitation leopard, tiger, and zebra. For the desk chair, consider one of those safari chairs that used to be called director's chairs or yacht chairs. I recommend the safari chair in black canvas with a black frame as economical—usually less than 15 dollars.

If your little tiger is too active, perhaps you might get him one of those modern plastic shell chairs—easy to wipe off, inexpensive to buy, and light in weight. The end table might be Dad's old army trunk, perhaps painted vibrant red, sunshine yellow, or pheasant orange. Paint the hinges of the trunk a contrasting color, perhaps black for real definition. If the lounge chair is covered in tiger naugahyde and the desk chair is a black safari chair, a combination of orange, lemon, chocolate, and white would work well as the decorating color scheme.

All walls can be painted sunny lemon with a white window trim and a white door. The bedcover can be bright orange corduroy. Bed pillows should be made of bright yellow, chocolate, and tiger naugahyde. (Naugahyde for all pillows—please! They get thrown on the floor.) Window curtains behind the tiger-upholstered lounge chair can be lemon (like the walls) or bright orange (like the bedcover). The rug on the floor can be either wool or acrylic of a tweedy chocolate and black mixture. The bulletin board can be chocolate felt with a frame covered in tiger naugahyde. And P.S.: All light fixtures and lamps can be made of the jungle's finest and least expensive wicker!

A Nursery for the Single-Family Home (House Plan #10, Bedroom Three)

A nursery in the single-family home should be furnished and decorated as cheerfully and as inexpensively as possible. It should be close to the master bedroom and as close to the second bathroom as possible. Consult Plan #8 in Chapter I to see the location of the nursery in relation to the master bedroom.

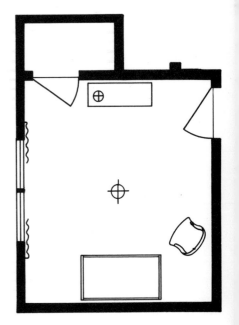

In nursery decoration, practicality comes first. The flooring in the room should definitely be vinyl, perhaps a sky blue with white and black flecks. Do not go for pink vinyl on the nursery floor even if the baby is a girl. Your next child might be a boy! Sky-blue vinyl is always safe. If the baby is a girl, you can paint the nursery walls a pale petal pink, which works well with sky blue as does sunny yellow. In fact, all colors—bright red, chocolate, and persimmon—look well with sky blue. The only color I never recommend for nursery decor is green, particularly that pale institutional green. Did you know that in hospital nursery decor, the color green is not used? It is believed by some people that green may affect the color of a baby's skin.

For wall decor, get lots of colorful animal prints or storybook prints. Window curtains should be washable white cotton. If you insist on a wall covering for the nursery, choose a washable one you can use on walls as well as ceilings. There are a number of balloon designs as well as designs featuring fairy-tale characters, animals, cookies, Raggedy Ann dolls, lollipops, trains, etc.

Chapter III

Your Budget and You

This book is not designed to tell you how to find signed pieces of French furniture for the best possible price, nor will we discuss the making of festoon blinds with silk tassels and shirred silk ruchings. Rather, my intent is to show that good decorating can be achieved within a budget, provided the family doing the decorating will use their ingenuity and invest the necessary patience, time, and energy. If all members of the family work together, decorating the home can be fun as well as inexpensive.

Something Old, Something New

Good decorating does not mean throwing the old away and buying everything new. Rather, it means taking the good of the old and combining it with the good of the new to create an exciting, warm, and personal interior within the home. Whenever I am called in to do a home-decorating job, the very first thing I do is take an inventory of everything within the home—a listing of all furniture, with sizes and finishes. Then I study the inventory carefully before I begin to draw and plan room layouts. A house, to be a home, must reflect the background and tastes of the family. I try to learn my client's background, likes and dislikes; only then do I begin planning room layouts. Into the room layouts go, first, the furnishings that have meaning. If Mrs. Brown has a dining room set that her grandmother left her, which is in good condition with the exception of a nick or two on the tabletop and with the exception of the upholstery on the seats of the dining chairs, I most certainly put her dining room set into my plans. After all, the tabletop can be refinished and the chair seats can be re-covered. Into the room plans, then, go all the furnishings still in good condition and which work scale-wise according to room sizes. Exchange not the old friend for the new! Why get rid of a good old dining table that is serviceable and attractive simply for the sake of having a new table? Why

get rid of your old comfortable sofa that has good proportions simply for the sake of having a new, modern wood-framed sofa? It doesn't make sense! Of course, if your sofa is completely out of proportion for your room and your sofa upholstery is completely gone and the frame of the sofa is weak and the feathers have started to come out of the cushions, then certainly it's time to put old man davenport out to pasture.

Use common sense when discarding old furniture and buying new. Don't be overemotional about the old club chair that was Grandpa's favorite. If its proportions are wrong or it's in bad condition and takes up one-fourth of your living room space, get rid of it. Grandpa would have wanted it that way.

I recently had a client for whom I decorated a small New York City apartment, using furnishings formerly from his home in the country. Not with the hand of God could I have utilized certain size club chairs and sofas within the living room of the gentleman's apartment. I finally managed to have my client understand the problem and buy new, more compactly designed upholstered furnishings. However, when it came to disposing of the original overstuffed pieces, he became emotional rather than logical and sent all the furniture to storage, where the pieces will sit for many years to come, collecting comfortable, overstuffed storage charges.

Rarely is it more costly to re-cover sofas and lounge chairs than it is to buy new. If you have a sofa in good condition and of good proportions, call in

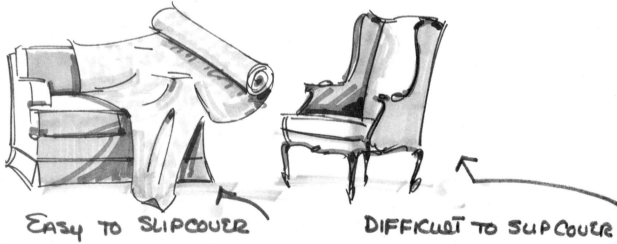

EASY TO SLIPCOVER   DIFFICULT TO SLIPCOVER

a local upholsterer for an estimate. He will have many fabric samples in a variety of colors for you to choose from, one of which certainly will go with your decorating scheme. When reupholstering sofa and lounge chairs, be certain to have arm caps made for your sofa arms. Caps save lots of wear and tear as well as soil. When the caps are soiled, send them out for cleaning or, if your sofa is covered in a washable quilted-cotton fabric, wash the arm caps yourself. The chart provides an accurate yardage guide for sofas, club chairs, and occasional chairs in case you buy your fabric from a source other than your upholstery man. You may be away on a trip and find the perfect fabric for your sofa or club chair. The yardage chart will tell you exactly how much you need.

On Slipcovering

Everyone should use slipcovers. In my own home, I use them from May until late September on all my upholstered sofas and chairs. Slipcovers are

YARDAGE CHART - Based on 50"w fabric

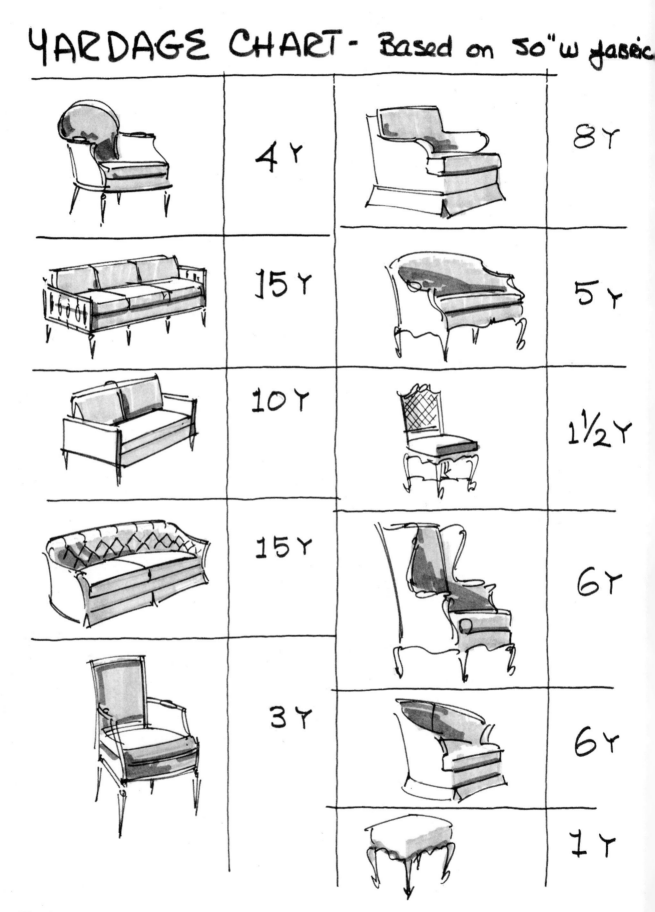

4 Y	8 Y
15 Y	5 Y
10 Y	1½ Y
15 Y	6 Y
3 Y	6 Y
	1 Y

easily made for square-back T-cushion lounge chairs and for Lawson-style armchairs, as well as for ottomans and square-arm and Lawson-arm sofas. More difficult to slipcover are fitted round-back club chairs, as the covers do not fit so snugly as they do on square-back chairs. Lounge chairs that have some exposed wood on their arms fall into the same category. Illustrated in the sketch are the easily slipcovered chairs and sofas as well as the more difficult pieces. The slipcover is instant decorating magic. It can change the character of a room in a matter of minutes. A client for whom I decorated a single-family home in the Harrisburg area of Pennsylvania had a rather formal living room. Her long sofa was covered in a creamy-beige cotton velvet that matched the draperies. The two club chairs that flanked the sofa were covered in a crewel fabric—russet and green tones on beige. She kept her beige and crewel look during the fall and winter months, but when springtime came, on went the yellow and green flowered-chintz slipcovers on the long sofa. On went the wide green and white striped cotton slipcovers on the lounge chairs. Up went the summer drapery, sunny lemon yellow with a valance of the same chintz used for the sofa. The sofa pillows also got the slipcover treatment—emerald-green zippered covers. The illustration shows the room before and after.

Inexpensive Foyer Decorating: Paint Your Own Stripes (House Plan #7)

For me, stripes are the common denominator of the decorating world. The stripe goes with absolutely everything. You can use a striped fabric on chairs with flowered-chintz fabric on your sofa, with plain fabric as drapery, as did my Harrisburg client with her summer slipcovers. A stripe can be used with a geometric-designed fabric or with a damask fabric or a floral fabric. A stripe with a print always works; a print with another print almost never does. It is as difficult to use two florals in one room as it is for a woman to wear a lilac-patterned skirt with a tulip-patterned blouse. Each must be used or worn alone!

In the course of a recent visit to a new residential community for which I served as interior-design consultant, I was asked by one of the homeowners, "Can we do anything with the plain, dead-white-painted foyer and hallway in our home to give it a little life?" Since she had used an overall floral fabric in her living room, I suggested that she paint three-inch-wide lemon stripes from ceiling to floor on the walls in her foyer and on the walls in the hallway to the bedrooms. Hers was exactly that foyer and hallway shown in house Plan #7. To get the striped effect, they cut eight-foot

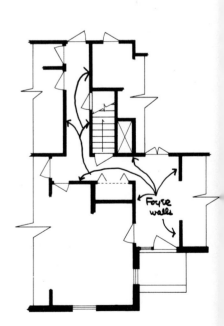

strips of brown paper which they masked to the walls in the hall from crown moulding to baseboard. The first 3 inches of wall space was left white; the next 3 inches was covered with one of the three-inch-wide strips of brown paper. The next 3 inches of space was left white and the next 3 inches covered with brown paper, and so on. The strips went alternating merrily along on the foyer and hallway walls. After all the strips had been applied to the wall surfaces, my client took cans of lemon spray paint and filled in all the white wall space. Before the spray painting was begun, both the crown moulding and the baseboard were covered with masking tape. The paint was left to dry overnight. When all the masked strips were removed, my friends had a beautiful alternating lemon-and-white striped foyer and hallway, at the cost of only the brown paper, the masking tape, and the lemon paint—much less expensive than wallpaper.

Old Furniture Can Look New

A retired Finnish couple I know have a most interesting house on an island off the coast of Florida. The house has been lovingly put together with a great deal of creative effort and a minimum of expense. In their dining room they used false beams, which they painted an antiqued blue-green. They made lamps out of driftwood. They created a coffee table from an old lobster trap; its top is made of glass. They cut the legs off an old dresser, thus lowering the chest. The wooden pulls on the drawers were replaced with old pewter hardware. The entire piece was painted an antique green to match the dining room beams and each drawer was outlined with a line of gold and a line of burnt red. *Voilà*—a handsome new room buffet.

73

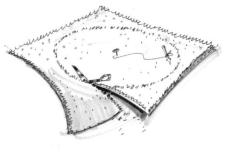

Save Your Old Rugs—A Budget Idea

Carpeting is one of the single most expensive furnishing items for the home, particularly if you go wall to wall in every room. For those who want to economize, try cutting down one of those old rugs you planned to throw away. If you have a 9-foot-by-15-foot rug that has some worn areas around the edges, consider cutting the carpet into an 8-foot-diameter area rug as shown in the illustration. You can draw your own circle onto the rug by tying a piece of chalk to one end of a four-foot piece of heavy string. The other end of the string is tied to a nail and the nail is tacked into the center of the carpet. Then simply pull the string tight and draw a circle. This gives you your 8-foot-diameter rug. With a pair of heavy scissors or with a carpet-cutting knife, cut around the chalk line you have drawn. To prevent the rug from fraying around the perimeter, bind it with some carpet-binding tape, available at your local rug or carpet store.

Contact Papers—A Decorating Bargain

Recently, during a Sunday supper party, Helene, my hostess, insisted that I inspect her newly decorated powder room. All the walls and the ceilings

had been covered with a delightful pink and candy-melon plaid contact paper. The hand towels were melon and pink. Sitting on the tank part of her white commode was a small apothecary jar filled with melon-colored soaps and a pink plastic tissue holder with white tissue. The plaid pink and candy-melon contact paper was also used to cover the outside of the metal wastebasket. Helene told me that she had created her powder room decor for less than 10 dollars. Since she already had the pink and melon towels, they were not part of her decorating costs.

Can Furniture Periods Be Combined?

Many homemakers are under the false impression that a home has to be done in a certain style. I can't tell you how many times I am asked how I decorated my own house. Was it in Spanish, or Italian provincial, or French, or modern, or Oriental, or Victorian? Unfortunately, and quite

disappointingly, I have to tell people that I did not plan it around any one style. A home can be decorated with furnishings from many design periods, provided the coordination of pieces is done with an eye toward comfort and scale. Furnishing periods can be coordinated but it should be done with some idea of style in mind. For example, a rattan chair would not be effective next to a French white and gold wood-framed and velvet-covered sofa. Likewise, a Victorian chair would not work well with French oval-back pull-up chairs. A Tiffany chandelier would be out of place hanging from the ceiling in a fruitwood-paneled French dining room, just as a bronze French clock would be out of place sitting in the corner of a Colonial kitchen.

Where, then, can periods be combined and how can this coordination be done economically and on a budget? My basic premise is that one need not throw away all the old furnishings when planning a new decor. Much can be saved of the old, even if you want a home with a modern overtone. A modern glass-top cocktail table on a stainless-steel base or on a bronze base works well and is most serviceable and practical with almost every style of furnishing. The sketch shows how a glass-top coffee table works with the decor in a traditionally planned Williamsburg living room. You can also see in another illustration how a glass-top table works with the decor in a family room with definite Spanish overtones in its furnishing.

Creating Interesting Wall Decor for the Budget-Minded

Family attics and storerooms can be a veritable treasure trove of decorating finds. Why not browse through Grandma's attic, or even your own, for

that matter. You're bound to find some interesting old pictures, wall plaques, medals—maybe even a model boat that you can mount on the wall above the sofa in your family room. If the frame on Aunt Matty's needlepoint flower picture is old and tarnished, give it a new coat of paint, in a color that picks up one of the colors in Aunt Matty's flowers.

The growing number of country antique stores and shops are proof of the value of the old. These shops sell everything from penny candies to old tea canisters to cracker boxes to flat irons to antique telephones to old copies of *Harper's Bazaar* and *Saturday Evening Post*. Remember—exchange not the old friend for the new!

Plants for Interior and Exterior Beauty

With the help of plants, cut flowers, and leaves, you can add instant, inexpensive beauty to your home. A row of geranium plants in clay pots at the

kitchen window. A large vase of rhododendron leaves in the fireplace. A bunch of fresh lemon leaves in an ordinary glass vase on a living room table or on a foyer console or on a dining room buffet. Potted plants and trees as inexpensive room dividers. An arrangement of fall leaves in the center of a dining table in the autumn. Pussy willows at the top of a staircase landing in early springtime. Popping yellow forsythia branches gracing the corner of a living room. Plants and branches and leaves bring instant color and beauty into the home.

Chapter IV

The Most Magical Decorating Tool—Color

The world is filled with color. Walk through a summer garden and note the different colors you see. The list will be staggering! Grass green, cosmos pink, cosmos white, lilac, delphinium blue, delphinium white, marigold orange, marigold lemon, hydrangea blue, hydrangea purple, aster pink,

It's Spring!

aster purple, snapdragon white, snapdragon lemon, snapdragon pink, sweet william blue, tulip red, talisman rose, nasturtium orange, buttercup yellow, petunia pink, bark brown, thorn green, birch white, fir green, laurel green, chestnut brown. Nature in all its beauty gives us many colors.

Picking a Color Scheme from the Season

Whenever I go into a house or an apartment, I look at the color scheme and immediately identify it with a season. A fall-season room would have creamy-beige walls, beige carpeting, copper-colored sofas, burnt-or-

Summer Flowers!

ange pillows, and olive-green lounge chairs. Spring rooms would feature sky-blue walls, white ceilings and door trims, emerald-green carpeting, daffodil-yellow upholstery on lounge chairs, and pale-forsythia-colored pillows on the emerald-green sofa. White walls, white drapery trimmed in icy blue, royal blue and white damask-covered sofas, royal-blue carpeting and bright-red pillows as accents would be found in a winter room. Then, for summer, country-garden chintz is used as drapery and as the upholstery material on lounge chairs and sofas. The walls in the summer rooms should be a pale yellow with white trim or sky blue with white trim or simply white. Each of the four sketches is appropriately marked for a season. Look at the rooms in your own home. Can you identify a season with each room?

Autumn Leaves!

Planning the Living Room Around
the Fall Season

Fall colors are restful and not so vibrant in tone and value as the summer colors, and many people find them easy to live with. I recently planned a family living room around the fall-season colors. The walls were painted a pale beige, the same beige used for the drapery and valance at the one living room window. The carpeting was a rich gold, the same gold color used for the accent pillows on a wide-wale sage-green corduroy sofa. Club chairs that pulled up to the sofa were covered in a chocolate and beige houndstooth check, and the two occasional chairs were covered in the same wide-

WINTER ICE

The Flower Test!

wale sage-green corduroy. In sum, the fall color scheme was beige, rich gold, sage green, and chocolate brown. The pictures above the sofa were matted in bright persimmon orange.

The Family Room—Perennial Springtime

If you like Colonial furniture and the used-brick and New England red barn look, your family room will most likely take on the autumn look, complete with stained-wood rocking chairs, braided rugs, and a black pot hanging from the inside of the fireplace. Others, however, prefer to go the springtime route in color. One homemaker once told me, "I'm forever in the kitchen/family room and I want this room to be as bright, gay and cheerful as possible." The family room planned for this young wife had a sky-blue vinyl floor. Kitchen cabinets were a white birch laminate. Counter tops were sky-blue laminated plastic, almost exactly the same color as the vinyl floor. The walls were covered in a gay country-floral-print washable wall covering, clusters of sky-blue and emerald-green flowers on a white background. The kitchen ceiling was covered with a washable vinyl wall covering called "Nantucket plaid"—sky blues and greens on a white background. This coordinated perfectly with the flowers in the wall covering used. Bright marigold-orange café curtains were double-hung at the windows on brass rings and rods. The sofa was covered in marigold-orange naugahyde, as were the seats of the stools that pulled up to the sky-blue laminated-plastic serving counter. For an accent color, crocus-yellow throw pillows were used on the sofa. Place mats used were lemon, napkins hot orange, and water glasses, sky blue hobnail!

Picking Your Favorite Color

Now is the time to use the color-picture test again to select your favorite color. Look quickly at a series of pictures or prints. Put into one pile those to which you react favorably. Discard the ones you don't like. From the first pile you will find a definite combination of color preferences. Perhaps blue and yellow are the predominating colors, or perhaps red, beige, and Wedgwood blue. The color-picture test will tell you in which direction your color interests go.

There is no set rule in determining one favorite color, as one's favorite may be a combination such as sky blue with buttercup yellow and emerald green, or mocha with sunny orange and champagne beige, or vermilion red with ebony black, crisp white, and charcoal gray, or copper with beige, or lime green with navy, or fern green with pomegranate red.

For women, this is comparable to the process of selecting a new dress, lipstick shade, or blouse. And men do the same thing when choosing a new necktie or shirt.

THE TOWEL TEST!

Another method I often use with clients to determine color preference is to examine their linen closets with respect to towel color. Towels are initially purchased with little thought of color coordination in mind. Rarely do people go to a towel counter in a department store and stop to think of their bathroom color scheme before buying. Towels are generally purchased on the basis of instinctive color preference. If a linen closet reveals a preponderance of towels in greens and blues, I can be pretty certain that the lady of the house prefers those colors over reds, pinks, and oranges. If the towels are all crisp whites, I know that the client will generally select a gay print with a white background instead of a printed fabric on a colored background. Lavenders, pinks, and pastels suggest that my client will want pastel tones in the master bedroom, foyer, powder bath, and master bath. The towel test generally works best with people who are not very decorating conscious. Those who are, however, will generally select towels to go with individual bathroom decor.

A wise husband is aware of his wife's favorite flower, for women have instinctive likes and dislikes about flowers. Some prefer yellow roses over red or pink. Others will buy white poinsettia plants at Christmas time instead of the red. There are women who prefer vases of lemon-yellow and white gladiolas over the red, fuchsia, and purple varieties. The woman who prefers yellow roses over red roses will most often dress in tones of lemon, white, beige, blue, and green. Her dress as well as her decorating tastes will run toward the soft tones and shades. A women with a red-rose taste will wear pinks, vivid strawberries, peach tones. Her decorating tastes will run toward startling and exciting fabrics, to contrasting color schemes and to new and exciting effects in interior design in general.

Vanilla Decorating—The Greige Way

I have seen many homes that have been decorated attractively and with great flair and color sense, all within the confines of a budget. I have seen

VANILLA DECORATING - WHY HAVE THIS ?

just as many decorated without budget restrictions that have no flair or color whatsoever. I call such homes "vanilla-decorated."

A vanilla-decorated home will have a beige or greige (a combination of beige and gray) carpet. The walls will be either beige, white, institutional green, or grayed-down blue, or a rosy beige. All fabrics used on sofas, lounge chairs and dining room chair seats, and all window hangings will be in the greige and rosy-beige tones. Not all fabrics, of course, will be solids. A greige-on-beige linen-damask pattern may be used on the sofa and a nubby-tweedy greigy-rose fabric may be used on the lounge chairs. Everything, but everything, however, is in the greige tones, and all the furniture finish, believe it or not, will be of the same walnut wood tone. The people who live in single-family houses decorated in this manner are living in an interior world devoid of color. Thank God they get out of

You can have this —

doors! Most people take the vanilla approach because they are afraid of making mistakes. But it is much better to make a mistake or two than to live in a colorless house interior. To avoid the vanilla-decorated home, try the "color is magic" approach. This doesn't mean you have to throw everything away. Start by buying some bright cerulean-blue and lemon pillows for that greige-on-beige damask sofa. Hang some bright chintz curtains at your windows. If your walls are beige, find a chintz with bright green, yellow, and blue flowers on a beige background. If your walls are spanking white, find a gay chintz with a white background. Be a little daring, and buy enough yardage of the drapery chintz to make slipcovers for your griegy-rose lounge chairs.

New draperies, slipcovered lounge chairs, and colorful throw pillows will take you and your family out of the woeful world of greige, and your vanilla-decorating days will be gone forever.

A word of caution and advice about all wood furniture in any room having the same stained tone: It is not necessary to match all the pieces. It is, in fact, as unnecessary as it is for a woman to match the color of her dress to the color of her shoes to the color of her bag to the color of her hat to the color of her gloves to the color of her shopping bag. A room needs contrast in furniture finishes. One of the first things I learned as a decorator was that every room needs a touch of black to be successfully decorated. This lesson came from my teacher and friend Leon Hegwood. It was his belief that a room, no matter how small, should have a touch of black. It might be the lacquer color of a coffee table or the black base of the lamp on the living room commode or simply the black frame on a picture hanging in a grouping above the sofa.

Every Room Needs a Touch of Black !

The Accessory Approach to a Color Scheme

Many women use the "accessory approach" to style. Their dresses, coats, and suits are basically in one of the neutral tones of beige, gray, black, or pale green, but—look at their accessories. The coat may be beige, but the handbag, gloves, hat, and shoes can be any color of the spectrum from vivid red to spicy orange to cerulean blue.

The "accessory approach" works just as well in the decoration of the house. Recently I worked with a young woman on the decoration of her two-story single-family home in upstate New York. All the walls in the living room

ACCESSORIES FOR THE HOME!

ACCESSORIES FOR THE WOMAN !

were painted a very soft, pale neutral blue. The fabric used on the sofa was a sky-blue nubby-chenille fabric, and the covering for two lounge chairs was a light-blue moiré. A pale-blue on sky-blue stripe, tone on tone, provided the covering on a love seat in the room as well as on the seat of the piano bench. At the windows, as overdrapery, the light-blue moiré fabric was hung with sheer white fiber-glass undercurtains. The entire room, including the carpeting, was thus decorated in sky and pale neutral blue, but the room fairly sang with the accessory colors: lemon yellow and shrimp. Lemon-yellow and shrimp pillows were used on the blue-chenille sofa. Hassock-style ottomans on casters covered in lemon naugahyde were used as pull-ups at the coffee table. An Oriental screen of shrimp-colored branches on gold paper framed in black lacquer was hung above the sofa. A cigarette table used between the lounge chairs was lacquered in lemon yellow. My client painted some old wood lamps with the same lemon lacquer she used on the cigarette table. The finished room was delightful.

The "accessory approach" can be effective and exciting, provided the accessory color or colors exist on more than just the pillows. This will never do the job. The accessory color or colors must be found elsewhere in the room—in the matting of pictures, in the design of the wallpaper used in the guest closet off the living room, or in the covering used on the hassock ottomans.

The advantages of accessory decorating are many. If my client tired of the shrimp and lemon accessory colors, she could change to a number of other color schemes at a minimum of expense—perhaps to sky blue with emerald green and chocolate. The pillows could be slipcovered with emerald-green and chocolate print fabric. The hassocks could be re-covered with chocolate naugahyde. The cigarette table and lamps could be sprayed with emerald-green lacquer. The Chinese scroll print over the sofa with its shrimp branches on gold paper could stay, since its colors work with chocolate and emerald green.

Starting Out with White

Recently I was talking with a young couple who were readying themselves to move into a new single-family home. They had practically no furniture of their own, except a bedroom suite, an odd chair or two, a wood dining table, and four bentwood dining chairs. The pregnant young wife was somewhat in a quandary because she had to tell the painters what color to paint the living room, dining room, kitchen, master bedroom, guest room, and nursery. Inasmuch as they had given no thought whatsoever to their future decorating plans, my immediate advice was to "start off with white." I told them to have all walls and ceilings in the foyer, living room, dining room, kitchen, guest room, and master bedroom painted white. White can always be easily painted over when their decorating plans were settled. I did tell them, however, to paint the walls in the nursery a clear, pale sunny lemon, the ceiling a flat white, and the woodwork white semigloss enamel. If the baby was a girl, the lemon walls would coordinate well with pink blankets as well as with pink and lemon printed curtains at the window. If the baby was a boy, the lemon walls would work equally well with soft blue blankets and soft blue window curtains.

SKY BLUE IS MY FAVORITE COLOR.....

The Neutral Colors

To almost everyone the neutral colors are beige, gray, greige, eggshell, white, off-white, and black. There are many shades of beige, gray, and white, each of which can be used as a successful background for any decorating scheme. Beige, gray, white, and black are not the only neutral colors. In fact, sky blue is the most neutral color. God was the first to use it, as the background for the Earth. Consider sky blue as the background color in your living room. It works well with emerald green. Try a decorating scheme of sky blue with vivid red, or sky blue with buttercup yellow or with chocolate. Sky blue is equally effective with lavenders and purples; sky blue and melons look well together on terraces, in family rooms, and on summer porches.

Other neutral colors are pale pinks and clear lemons. A neutral pink or lemon can be achieved by the addition of lots of white pigment to the basic color. A pale-pink background is great with reds, vivid blues, hot yellows, chocolates, emeralds, Kelly greens, paprika oranges, and velvety purples. Lemon is a clear and sunny background color for chocolate and mocha browns, bright reds, delphinium blues, and geranium pinks. When selecting a neutral color for any room in your home, consider not only white and beige, but also my favorite sky blue, pale pink, or clear lemon. Use any of the colors for wall surfaces with a flat, pure-white ceiling. Have all your door surfaces, baseboards, and window casings, if they are wood, painted with washable white semigloss enamel.

A Few Closing Words on Color

There is a host of colors to choose from. Never limit yourself to the beiges. I have always believed that black and white were colors, and I use them very often in my work. I love a room completely decorated in black and white, with a third color, perhaps shocking pink, hot tomato red, emerald green, or sunny yellow. Note the color sketches of the two rooms decorated in black and white. One features black and white with red as the third color. The other is black and white with cerulean blue.

In selecting a color scheme, never restrict your thinking to the vanilla-decorating tones, nor should you restrict your thinking to the three primary colors—red, yellow, and blue—or to the three secondary colors—green, orange, and purple. Look around you and choose from all the many tones, hues, and values that are found in nature's palette.

Chapter V

Ways with Walls and Ceilings

Paint goes a long way toward giving a room in your home a new and bright look. A word of caution about paint—never select paint on the basis of its liquid color in the can. Remember, dark-color paints dry light; light-color paints dry dark. Always ask to see a dry sample of the paint you select, for the true color cannot be seen in the liquid form. Another point to remember: Woodwork surfaces covered with a gloss or a semigloss paint are easily washed. Most flat paints for wall surfaces are made with a water base. Walls painted with a water-base paint are not easily washed, while those painted with an oil-base paint are washable. While oil-base paints are more costly than the water-base paints, they are, in the end, very much worth the extra initial investment.

How To Make a Small Room Look Larger with a Coat or Two of Paint

I recently decorated a single-family two-story house in upstate New York. The house had suffered minor fire damage prior to its being sold to my clients. They wanted to restore the house to its former beauty and enlarge a room or two and make it livable and comfortable for themselves and their three young children, two boys and a girl.

On the upper level at the front is a bedroom to be occupied by the daughter of the house. When I first saw this charred and smoke-damaged room, it looked extremely small and closed in. My client was afraid that the room would not be large enough to hold twin beds as well as the dresser, desk, and lounge chair. In plan, however, the room was indeed ample and could house all of the necessary furniture and belongings. What had confused my client was the darkness and dreariness of the blackened walls and ceilings. The dark colors made it appear much smaller than it really was. Now the room has been opened up by a coat of fresh pale-pink oil-base flat paint on the walls. The ceiling has been painted white, as have the wood window mullions, the door surfaces, and the built-in bookcase units to the left and right of the beds. The backs of the built-in bookcases were lined with the same fabric used for the bedspreads. The old bedspreads were used; fabric for the backs of the bookshelves came from yardage on hand. The avocado-green rug had been the dining room area rug in their former home. When moving from one single-family home to another, my clients were creative yet cost conscious. Why buy a new rug or carpet for their daughter's room in the new house if the avocado-green carpet from the dining room in their old home would work? And it happens that avocado and pink make a most exciting color combination. The rug looked beautiful. Remember that a dark-painted room will appear larger if the room is repainted a light color. This particular room became large with pale pink on the walls and bright white on the ceilings. In general, if the rooms in your home are small, do not paint walls with dark paints such as bottle greens, navy blues, mustards, reds, browns, blacks, or deep purples or plums. Walls

and ceilings in small rooms should be painted with light and bright clear colors—white, pale sky blues, clear lemons, frosty greens, or petal pinks. While the pastel neutral colors open up space, they do not work so well as the standard white.

How to Make a Large Room More Intimate and Cozy

In order to make a large room appear less barnlike or less spacious than it is, take the opposite approach to that used for the small, closed-in room. Do not go for light white or pastel lemon or frosty mint green or clear sky blue. In a large room, use dark colors such as bottle green, deep mustard, navy blue, plum, dark gray, deep maroon, red, or chocolate brown. Few people have the large-room problem, but for those of you who have one of those old single-family homes with the big rooms and high ceilings, you know how to treat your walls colorwise, if you want your rooms to be more intimate and cozy. Having said that, I must confess that if I had a home with

a large living and dining room, I'd make the rooms more intimate with comfortable sofa and chair groupings, pretty crisscross white curtains at the windows, bright-colored rugs, and lots of picture groupings on the walls. In fact, I'd even paint the walls with a bright, clean color—white or pale blue. The more spacious I can make a room look, the better I like it. Perhaps my attitude comes from being a city dweller for the past twelve years, while secretly wanting to live in the country in a nice big country home.

The rule for the painting of large rooms in order to make them more intimate and cozy is use dark colors, not light.

On Painted Ceilings, or How To Raise the Roof

Many people like to paint their ceilings a different color from that of their walls. Painted ceilings can be effective in decorating, but they must be handled carefully. If you have a small bedroom in your home with white walls and you want to paint the ceiling dark green to match the color of the carpeting on the floor, you may do so, but remember—a ceiling that is painted a darker color than the walls appears lower than it really is. I'm afraid I would not want to be the person sleeping in the small bedroom that had white walls and a dark-green ceiling. I would think that the ceiling was practically on top of me! In my early camp days, I never liked bunk beds, either on the top or on the bottom. When I slept on top, I thought the ceiling would cave in on me. When I slept on the bottom, I thought the bed above would come down on me. Remember, dark colors on ceilings lower the roof! Light colors on ceilings raise the roof!

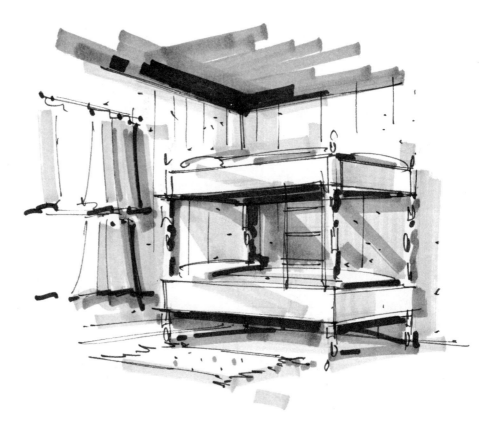

On Painting the Long Hallway

The long hallways are often found in Vermont farmhouses, or Maine brick houses, or Kentucky white frame houses. In such houses, the long hall is on the second floor directly at the top of the stairs and runs from one end of the house to the other with bedroom doors opening on either side. To solve the long-hall problem, I suggest that a dado be installed on the walls on both sides of the hall. The dado is a wall design that adds great interest to overall decor. I use it often in foyers, living rooms, dining rooms, and bedrooms, as well as in long hallways. The dado, sometimes called the "wainscot," is a section of wall starting from the floor and going up the wall some 32 inches. It includes the baseboard and ends with the chair rail. The baseboard and chair rail are elements by themselves in design, but together and with the wall space between, they make up the dado. In the long hallway illustrated the dado has been painted white and goes along the hallway as well as around the far end wall on which there is a window. The walls above the dado have been painted a cheerful lemon yellow. The

bedroom doors are white semigloss enamel, as are the louver shutters installed on the end window. To visually shorten the length of the hallway, a black and white striped vinyl floor has been laid horizontally from one wall to the other, using nine-inch-square tiles. A row of nine-inch-square white tiles was laid; then a row of nine-inch-square black tiles was laid. A decorating plus results from the use of wall decorations in the form of family snaps and photographs matted in emerald green and framed in black.

Should Entry Doors and Closet Doors Be Painted To Match the Walls of a Room?

Many times I am asked how closet doors in a bedroom should be painted. Should the entry door to a bedroom be the same color as the room's walls? The answer depends on the individual rooms involved. If a bedroom is small and has two closets on one wall, a bathroom door on a second wall, and the entry door on the third wall, definitely paint all the doors the same color as the walls. If, however, on one wall in the bedroom there is an entry door that balances a closet door, I would paint the entry door and the closet door with white semigloss enamel. The wall surface between the two doors as well as all walls in the room might be painted pale mint green or champagne beige or any color you might wish—a color that, of course, coordinates with your room's decor. The window mullions and baseboard in the bedroom with a white closet door and a white entry door should definitely be painted with white semigloss enamel. The illustrations show both a balanced and an unbalanced bedroom-door situation. The room with unbalanced doors has been painted the same color in entirety, doors included. Be certain to use a semigloss paint on the door surfaces. Doors get much handling and their surfaces should be washable.

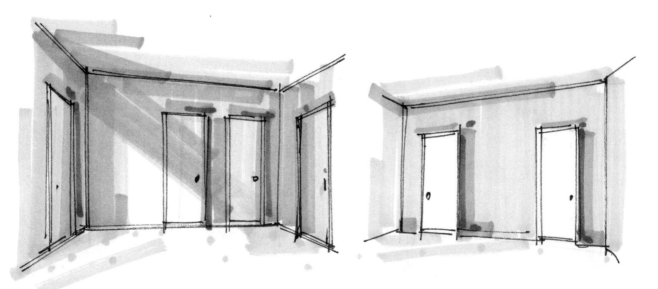

Paint Doors as Walls..   Paint Doors white....

What About Wallpaper?

One of the most effective ways to make a decorating splash is with wallpaper. There are thousands of different wallpapers. There are wallpapers that have been resistane-treated; there are washable wall coverings, both canvas-backed and paper-backed. "Resistane-treated" means that the papers "resist" stain and are washable. By "wall coverings" I mean wall vinyls. Wall vinyls come in rolls as do wallpapers. Wall vinyls come in hundreds and thousands of patterns and colors and are very practical and easily maintained. They are, however, in most cases more expensive than ordinary wallpapers or resistaned papers. In all my commercial decorating work—interiors for hotels, motels, restaurants, etc.—I always use washable vinyl wall coverings for their durability and ease of maintenance.

How To Figure the Number of Wallpaper Rolls You Need

To determine exactly the number of rolls you require, measure the perimeter of your room—the distance around the four walls. After you measure the perimeter, measure your ceiling height, the height from the wood baseboard to the finished ceiling line. Multiply the height of your room by its perimeter. This gives you the square feet in your room. Divide that figure by 30. The answer to your division problem will be the number of rolls of wallpaper or wall covering you require. There are actually 36 square feet of paper in every single roll. You cannot, however, divide by 36, because you have to allow for cutting and waste.

Next, measure your windows and doors, multiply width by height, and divide by 30 to determine how many rolls would be needed to cover them up. Deduct that rollage figure from your wallpaper count. Buy only the wallpaper rollage you require.

If you plan to do your own wallpapering, get a wallpapering kit at your local paint store—and read the section on "Hanging Your Own Wallpaper." Study the wallpapering directions carefully and start practicing on a closet first. If you do not make it as a wallpaper hanger, only the closet paper will be lost. Believe me, the art of wallpapering takes practice and patience.

CAN YOU HANG YOUR OWN WALLPAPER?

Yes. What you need first are:

1. Patience.
2. Ingenuity.
3. Common sense.

The supplies you need are:

1. Paste brush—buy two 5-inch or 6-inch nylon paint brushes.
2. Two one-gallon pails, one for mixing paste and one for water.
3. An eggbeater or some other kind of stirrer.
4. A yardstick.
5. A small 1-inch or 2-inch wooden roller.
6. A pair of shears (scissors).
7. A paper sweep.
8. A sponge.
9. Paste—a wheat paste is good for paper. Use vinyl paste for vinyl wall coverings, canvas-backed for paper-backed.
10. A plumb bob.
11. A ladder.
12. A razor blade, single edge, for trimming the paper.
13. A straightedge, at least 3 feet long.

First, mix your paste to a heavy, sweet-cream consistency until the paste is free of lumps—no lumps permitted. You can mix the paste with either hot or cold water. Most good paperhangers mix the paste with lukewarm water to prevent hand chapping.

A wallpaper table has to be set up with legs (you can use sawhorses with a plywood top). The table should be about 5 feet long by 3 feet wide.

Unroll your paper and check your pattern to be certain you received what you wanted and ordered from your wallpaper store. Do this when the paper arrives at your home. Once the paper is unrolled, place one roll on the table. Check to see which is the top and which is the bottom. This is marked on the selvage of the paper, generally with an arrow.

Next, measure the height of your wall, from baseboard to crown moulding or to ceiling. If you have no moulding around your room add some 5 inches or 6 inches to the measure you get. These 5 or 6 inches are important as they serve as security against cutting the paper too short for the wall. There are 15 running feet of paper in a roll 28 inches wide. There are 21 running feet of paper in a roll 18 inches wide. Most commercial papers today are 21 inches wide. Most hand prints are 27 to 28 inches wide.

Now that you have your height plus the security inches and you have unrolled one sheet, take out your trusty scissors and make the fatal cut. Cut your measured height. Next, unroll a second strip, lay it next to the first strip without cutting, to be certain it corresponds designwise with the first strip. If the design corresponds, cut at the same point. Continue with strip after strip until you have cut enough for the entire room. Cut pieces shorter, naturally, for all surfaces above doors and windows.

At this point, you may think that wallpapering is a great operation. Believe me, it takes only a few minutes to do the unrolling, and a few extra minutes, maybe a half hour, to cut the lengths—a half hour, that is, for a small room.

Turn all strips face down so that you look only at the back of the wallpaper.

Before putting paste on the back of the paper, find the starting point for hanging on your wall. Always start hanging paper at the farthest point from your entry door and work both walls—left to right and right to left—back to the point of entry. Measure from the starting point, the farthest corner from entry, the width of a sheet of paper and make a pencil mark high on the wall. Allow a small amount for wrapping of corners.

Place your plumb bob or level at the pencil mark, and at the bottom of the plumb bob make a second mark. Connect the two marks. This gives you a perfectly vertical line.

Apply paste to the top half of your first sheet for approximately 5 feet, then fold down halfway so that the design comes face up. Then paste the bottom section of the first sheet, and fold over so that the bottom portion of the paper faces up. Selvages should line up top and bottom.

You are now ready to trim the paper with a straightedge. Be careful not to cut any more than the selvage. There are two selvages on each roll of wallpaper, a right and a left.

Now that the paper is trimmed and your tools (sweeper, scissors, roller, wet sponge) are on your ladder or on your person, you are ready to hang your first sheet of paper, working from the drawn line to the farthest corner. Hang from the first line you created after measuring your design width and dropping your plumb bob. Hang from top down! Open the top section slowly, so as not to tear or split the paper. Lay it on the wall leaving a few inches over the top (on moulding or ceiling) and take your paper sweep and smooth out the paper so that it is tight to the ceiling or crown moulding. Press gently but firmly and sweep out all air so that the paper lies flat on the wall. Now take your shears and gently score into corner or at crown moulding. This will give you the mark where excess paper is to be cut with scissors. Lift the paper a few inches and cut on the scored line at ceiling. Take a clean sponge and wash excess paste off the ceiling or moulding, as well as off the paper.

You may now get off the ladder and open the bottom half of sheet, repeat the same process and score and cut by the base line. You have now hung your first sheet of paper.

If you're not exhausted by this time, begin again, paste, trim, hang, score, cut, roll seams, and wash. Your second sheet must be butted against the first sheet. This is done securely with a roller. The only time you make another level and plumb bob mark is when you start from another corner out. Normally, you do this four times in a room. If you should reach a corner and you have only half a sheet, measure the amount and add a half inch to allow for variation in the corner, in case it is crooked.

On Other Ways To Treat Walls—and Ceilings

There are a host of wall treatments that can enhance the decor in your rooms, treatments other than paint and wallpapers and wall vinyls. There are burlap wall coverings; there is cork; there is plywood; there are fabrics; there are felts; there are slates; there are hard-surfaced vinyl flooring materials that can be used for walls as well as floors; there are bamboo shoots; there are grasses of all sorts, in paper and in vinyl. There are thousands of new ways with walls. There are thousands of colors.

Walnut Shells and Paints on Rough-Textured Ceilings

A young wife I know who lives in Seattle devised an interesting way of creating a rough-textured ceiling finish. In her family room, the ceiling

surfaces between imitation beams were flat white. The flat surfaces on the ceiling just didn't belong with the beams. My friend went to the local paint store and bought an oil-base flat paint and a pound or two of walnut shells, ground the consistency of coarse sand. Into the white paint went the ground walnut shells! With a paint brush and a roller, she painted all the flat ceiling surfaces between the beams with her walnut-shell-and-paint combination. The result was a rough-textured ceiling that greatly enhanced the appearance of the room.

This would work as well on walls. I can see one rough-textured painted wall in a living room/dining room combination. The wall dividing the dining room from the kitchen might very attractively be painted with a rough walnut-shell-textured gold paint, sky blue, brown, or any color that would enhance your living room/dining room decor.

Mirror, Mirror on the Wall

Mirrored walls can be most effective. A mirrored wall can be used to create the illusion that a room is wider or longer than it really is. In the illustration, I have shown how a dining area became larger solely with the use of a mirrored wall. The wall dividing the dining room from the kitchen was

entirely sheet-mirrored from baseboard to cornice moulding. A drop-leaf table was used in the dining room, set against the mirrored wall. When the table was in its half-round state, set against the wall, it appeared fully round. The lighting fixture in this dining room was a half-round sconce, mounted on the mirror. The sconce looked as if it were a fully round hanging chandelier. It also provided adequate lighting for the dining area when the table was pulled out from the wall and opened to its full dimension. The half-round folding-leg table could also be used for buffet dinners at home.

Mirrored walls should be used discerningly and should reflect something attractive. I recall once visiting a home in Scarsdale, New York, in which a lawyer friend and his wife had used a complete mirror wall in their entry foyer. The mirror made the foyer look wider, but it reflected only the doors of the guest coat closet and the powder room. The mirror wall in this case was not used to advantage. I helped my friends overcome the unattractiveness of their entry foyer by suggesting that they install mouldings to create panels on the two door surfaces. The mouldings they used are shown in the sketch. The upper and lower panels were covered with a pale-lemon and mint-green striped wallpaper. The center panel was painted mint green and to the middle of the round panel a three-inch shiny-brass round

doorknob was applied. The surfaces around the door panels were painted with white semigloss enamel as were the door bucks, or frames. When the door decorating was completed, the mirrored foyer wall had something pretty to reflect!

I Like Stripes

For me, the color sky blue and the stripe are the two decorating common denominators. The stripe works with geometric-printed fabrics; it works with floral-printed fabrics; it works with damask-designed fabrics; it works with any style of furniture. In one of my recent decorating projects, I used a royal-blue and white striped wallpaper on the headboard wall in a young man's bedroom. I used the stripe, a ticking stripe, with bright red carpeting, royal-blue bedspreads and black-lacquered furniture. On the striped wall over the beds were hung colorful travel posters matted in bright red and framed in black. You can see that the stripe is a common denominator with pictures. Pictures can easily be hung on a striped wall, whereas pictures hung against a floral-patterned wallpaper get lost among the bouquets and the branches.

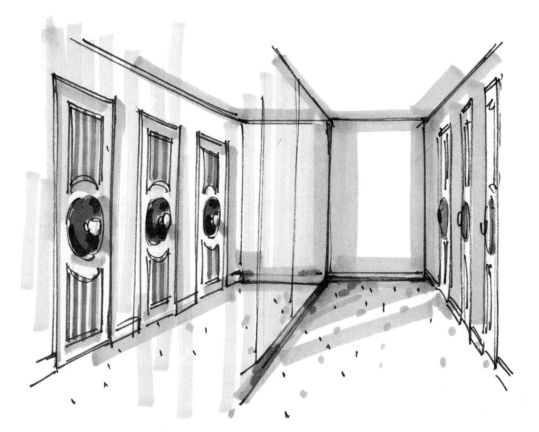

Murals Are Here To Stay

There are many attractive scenic papers and scenic vinyl wall coverings on the market. There are Georgian, Oriental summer house, early-American, Roman, and fishing-village scenics. These designs come in panels. There are four-, five-, six, seven-, and eight-panel scenics. If you work with the eight-panel design, you apply panels one to eight consecutively, then begin with panel one again. All panels connect and have been designed to fit together. If you want to use a scenic design in the foyer or on the dining room walls, or on the headboard wall in the master bedroom, find out from your wallpaper store the width of each scenic panel, as well as the height. Figure out how many panels you require by measuring your wall.

I am particularly partial to scenic-designed wallpapers in the dining room of the single-family home. If you are early-American-oriented, why not try an attractive Salem, Boston, or Jamestown mural above a dado in your dining area or dining room. The mural starts directly above the chair rail and covers the wall surfaces to the ceiling cornice moulding. You will most likely lose the top or the bottom sections of your mural panels if you install

the mural above a chair rail. I have shown two rooms in my illustrations. One sketch shows a dining room in house Plan #1. The second is of the dining area in Plan #8. Only the dividing wall between the dining room/ kitchen in Plan #8 has been treated with a mural and a dado.

Or you can paint your own mural. I have known a number of young men and women who have created and painted mural designs for their own homes. If you are your own muralist, you can be certain the one you create for your own home will be one of a kind!

Chapter VI

On Floors and Floor Coverings

There are literally hundreds of ways with floors. Whether you are moving into a newly constructed home or into an old Connecticut farmhouse, there will be a time when you see your home in the nude—without floor covering, window treatments, furniture, lighting fixtures, or accessories. It will be up to you to dress the naked room in the manner to suit your personal tastes as well as your pocketbook.

Covering the bare floors will generally require the largest portion of your budget if you go for wall-to-wall carpeting, or for wall-to-wall decorative vinyl. There are, however, many inexpensive ways to cover your naked floors if you use imagination. In this chapter, we shall show how to make your own fur area rug, how to cover your staircase with carpet samples, how and where to use inexpensive jute and hemp rugs, how to achieve a decorative look on your rumpus room floor with paint.

One of the most important things to consider before selecting the covering for any floor is use. Floors are subject to varying amounts of traffic. You should, for example, select a durable material for the kitchen/family room floor, perhaps vinyl asbestos tile (9-inch black and white squares laid on the diagonal). Or perhaps terra-cotta quarry tile. Similarly, a forest-green carpet for the living room is to be preferred over light beige. Gumdrop and chocolate stains are less visible on forest green.

Cotton shag rugs are easily washable. Use them in children's rooms and bathroom areas. Many people prefer the new acrylic carpeting over all wool-face varieties. Before making the investment in carpets and/or vinyls, study the use of each floor surface before selecting its covering. Let your floor remain naked until you are certain of its proper clothing.

Carpeting

Carpeting is one of the most costly items of furnishing for the home. Carpet ads stress its luxurious quality. They show that life can be beautiful with carpeting—ladies in hostess gowns dancing on carpeted floors, gentlemen in smoking jackets leisurely sipping a Scotch with one hand and feeling the plush carpeting with the other. There is one well-known series of ads that equates your name on the door with a carpet on the floor. I admit carpeting is expensive, even though I don't sit in a cozy leather lounge chair by my fireplace sipping Scotch and stroking my wall-to-wall carpeting. The advantages of wall-to-wall carpeting are many. Wall-to-wall carpeting unifies space, particularly in small homes. I would recommend it in the living room/dining room houses to create the feeling of oneness, provided, of course, that's what you want.

Wall-to-wall carpeting is also to be recommended as a covering for wood floors in poor condition, too poor to do much about. It also works well in two-story homes. Carpeting might be installed on the stairway up as well as in the upstairs hallway, to cut down the noise.

Wall-to-wall carpeting is installed generally by what is known as the "tackless method." Tackless strips are long pieces of wood that run around the perimeter of a room. These strips are installed before laying the underpad-

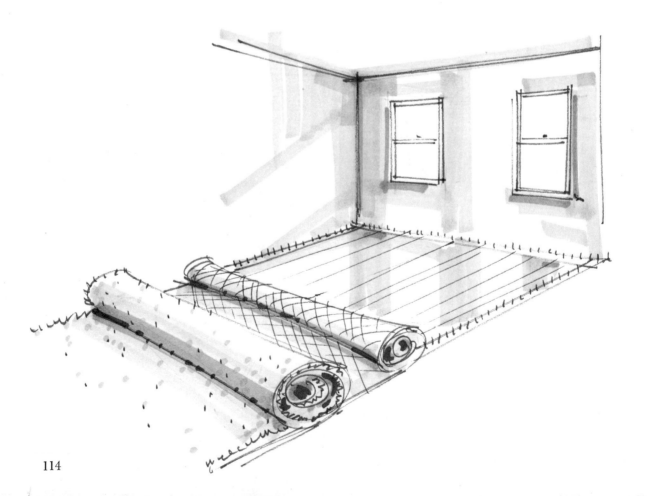

ding and before stretching the carpet. You should never see nails holding down wall-to-wall carpeting. The carpeting is stretched and kept in place by the tackless strips. The tacks on the stripping pop their pointed ends up to grab and hold tight to the back of a broadloom wall-to-wall carpet. The illustration shows a piece of tackless stripping and its general method of installation.

Wall-to-wall carpeting is the best answer for floors in living rooms that have many irregularities in the floor plan. For example, I recently put wall-to-wall carpeting in the home of a client in Buffalo. The room in which the carpeting was used had a fireplace in the center of the end wall, complete with a large hearth that projected into the room. To the left and right, respectively, of the fireplace was a square bay that projected some 36 inches. At the front of the room was a full bay window. In addition, there were five heating grates in the floor. Area rugs in the room described and illustrated would have been most unsightly and confusing. The wall-to-wall carpeting method was the best in this case, the carpeting being installed and fitted around the fireplace hearth, into the two 36-inch-square bays, into the front bay and around the heating grates.

For the schoolboy of the family, I would suggest a Tartan plaid wall-to-wall carpeting in his room. A plaid carpet in block form helps make a small

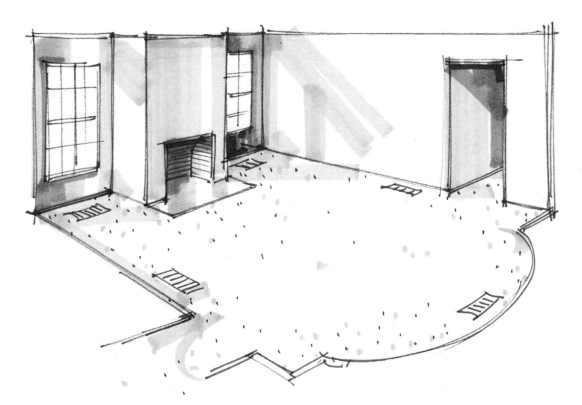

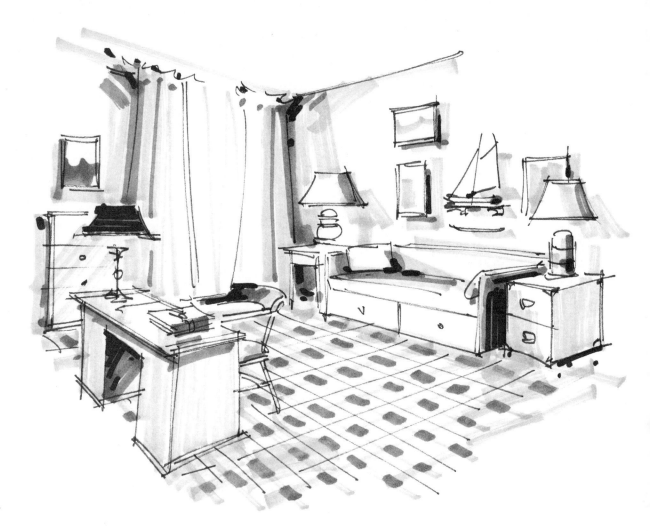

room look larger. The lines in the Tartan run both vertically and horizontally, giving added length as well as width to a room.

If cost is a factor or if you're concerned about wear and tear, forget the Tartan carpet and go for a vinyl floor, or a washable cotton shag laid directly on the wood flooring.

Carpeting for the Master Bedroom

There is no doubt about it—most women prefer wall-to-wall carpeting. This is especially true in decorating the living room and the master bedroom. However, in the decoration of living room/dining room houses, the client may want to use wall-to-wall carpeting for the living room area only and practical vinyl tile for the dining area. In other cases, when decorating the living room/dining room combination, a young wife will select an area rug for the living room and an area rug for the dining space. The

area rug used in the living room will be laid so as to permit a 12- to 16-inch border of wood flooring to show. The dining-space area rug can be oval or round, or even rectangular, depending on the shape of the dining table.

While many women might prefer large area rugs for their living room/ dining room combinations, they will surely insist that the master bedroom have wall-to-wall carpeting. Women in general like soft tones in the master bedroom, and the colors usually selected are shades of white, beige, light blue, or celadon green. I believe the woman of the family should decide the decor for the master bedroom. If light pink is her choice, let the master bedroom be decorated in pale pink. Many is the time I have had a client say, "Oh, I can't use pink in the master bedroom. It wouldn't be fair to Bill," or "I would love to use lavender and peach in the bedroom, but don't you think it's too feminine?" Sure, pink is a feminine color. So are lavender and peach. They are also great colors for a master bedroom. The master bedroom should definitely be directed to the tastes of the lady of the home, for she uses and enjoys it more than any other. This is the room in which she finds quiet from the children, uses to make up and to dress. Gentlemen, when it comes to your office or your den or your rumpus room, you may set the decorating concept. But let your wife have her way in the bedroom.

On Area Rugs

Area rugs are great definers of space, and are especially good on beautiful wood floors. When something is beautiful, I hate to cover it up! Area rugs work well in the living room space of the living room/dining room combination home. They are easily laid and, like carpeting, should be laid over a padding, never directly on the bare wood flooring. The padding standard I recommend is 52-ounce rubberized lining. Padding makes the rug softer to walk on and gives it a longer life-span. Unlike wall-to-wall carpeting, an area rug can be laid directly on the floor without the help of a professional carpet layer. Area rugs bound on all four sides therefore are less expensive from the installation point of view.

If you are considering an area rug for your living or dining room, measure the size of the room to determine what size rug you require. Perhaps your living room will take a 12-foot by 15-foot rug or a 9-foot by 12-foot rug or a 15-foot-square rug. Your dining room may require a 9-foot-diameter round or a 10-foot oval rug. I like to see rectangular area rugs laid in a living room of a size to permit a 12-inch border of wood flooring to show.

There are many kinds of area rugs. The rugs are not necessarily one color in their entirety, although solid-color area rugs can be purchased for less money than those with contrasting colored or sculptured borders. A word of caution about area rugs; They should be large enough to accommodate all the furniture. The back legs of the chair as well as the front legs should be sitting on the rug, never the front legs only.

Area rugs under dining tables should also be large enough to accommodate the table as well as the chairs when they are occupied. I recall once seeing a beautifully decorated dining area that had as its flooring a white Renaissance marbleized vinyl. In the middle of the dining area on top of the flooring was a sculptured-border oval area rug. This magic carpet, however, was only magic for the table and chairs when the chairs were unoccupied. The rug was far too small, for when the chairs were being used, the back legs would be off the rug and would rest on the marbleized vinyl. This dining area was planned for the table and chair setup, but nobody thought about people.

On Smaller Area Rugs

An area rug can be of any size: 9 feet by 12 feet, 12 feet by 15 feet, 4 feet

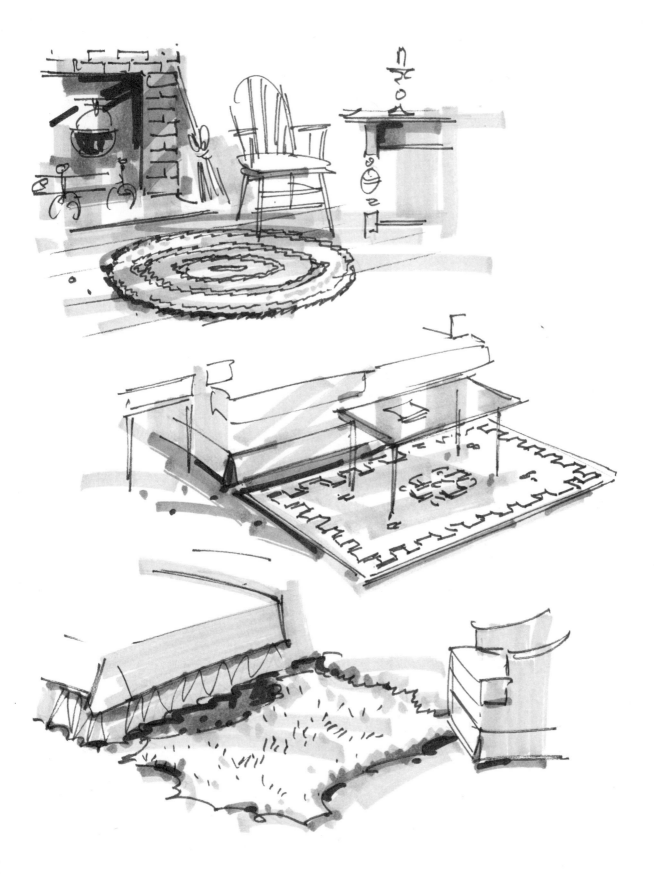

by 5 feet, or 3 feet by 4 feet. Small area rugs are delightful decorating touches in a living room, bedroom, family room, or, for that matter, in any room of the home. Why not try a braided area rug in your Colonial kitchen or an Oriental rug under your coffee table or an imitation fur rug at each side of the double bed in the master bedroom? In my own living room, I have used a beigey flaxen-color goat-hair rug under my glass-top coffee table.

How To Make Your Own Fur Rug

I have always wanted a great animal-fur rug, perhaps a tiger complete with head, or a polar bear, or a lion, to lay on the floor in my home. Unfortunately, every time I have priced such a rug, I've found it way out of

my range. Recently I met a young lady from Maine who had a great idea about fur rugs. This young mother of two teenage boys bought old fur coats at rummage sales. She removed the linings and cut the skins into eight-inch squares. She told me that the skins had to be cut with a razor blade on the hide side, not on the fur side, to avoid cutting the fur itself. She then sewed the squares together with an overcast stitch. "Stitching furs together with an overcast stitch takes a long time," she said. It is better, I understand and as she explained, to stitch twill tape around the perimeter of all squares. You can stitch the twill tape to the fur on a machine. After each square has been stitched with a perimeter of twill tape, start sewing the twill tapes together. It is easier to stitch twill tapes together than it is to sew hides together by means of the overcast stitch plan, since a needle doesn't go

My Dream.... ....○

through hides very easily. One day I'm going to try a fur rug made with eight-inch squares of fur cut from old coats. I think a rug combining all furs together would be a most exciting decorative addition to the floor in my living room. Perhaps I'll make my rugs of triangles instead of squares!

You Can Make Your Own Fur Rug!

On Oriental Rugs

Oriental rugs can be most attractively used in the single-family home or in any home, for that matter. They are very much in vogue today, and there are many people I know who would give their eyeteeth to have back the Orientals they once threw away!

I recall shopping recently with one of my clients for an Oriental rug to be used on the floor of her beige-toned dining room. We were accompanied on our shopping tour by my client's mother, who made this comment when she discovered we were looking for a good buy on an Oriental rug: "You

know, Joyce, some 30 years ago your father and I had Oriental rugs in our home. We gave them away because they went out of style."

Oriental rugs have never been out of style! They took a back seat in the minds of some people because they were identified with Great Grandfather's drawing room and Grandmother's parlor and with the very old chateaux of Europe. There is nothing more beautiful in a dining room, living room, or bedroom than a handsome Oriental rug. Oriental rugs cannot be used with floral chintz fabrics or with geometric-patterned wallpapers. They work best with rooms painted a solid color and with tone-on-tone damask fabrics. I love a rich red Oriental rug in a room with pale blue walls, a white ceiling and white window trim. I love to see red leather on the seats of dining chairs that sit on an Oriental rug. The color schemes for a room that features an Oriental rug must be built up around the color shades and tones in the rug itself. Striped fabrics and striped wallpapers look great in rooms that have Oriental rugs on the floor. Remember, the stripe will always be the decorating common denominator.

Painting the Floors in the Playroom or Rumpus Room

Not much is said today about painted floors. Years ago, people used to paint their soft-wood interior floors as often as they painted the flooring on their outside veranda. The veranda or porch floor was most often painted battleship gray or bottle green. The interior floors might have been brown, beige, black, or even one of the pastel tones of blue, yellow, pink, or green. Today, what with most new flooring being laid in a square-parquet design and not in a strip-board arrangement, people very rarely, if ever, paint their floors. Everyone seems to like the stained-wood flooring, be that flooring dark walnut or natural finish. There is a room in the house, however, that you might consider giving a coat or two of a high-gloss paint and that room is the basement playroom or rumpus room. In the design and decorating of a home I planned a year ago, I specified a painted floor for the playroom. The paint was actually applied to concrete, not to wood. The concrete was painted a bright lacquer red and was later spattered, first with black paint and, after drying, with white paint. The painted concrete floor was attractive, colorful, practical, and much less expensive than asphalt tile, vinyl tile, carpeting, or wood parquet. Consider paint for the concrete floor in your basement if your funds are limited and you want to create a lot of look on only a little!

On Jute and Hemp Rugs

Jute and hemp rugs are being used very often today, as they are effective and inexpensive. The only thing I don't like to do is walk on the hard and prickly jute or hemp in bare feet. When I was in summer camp, I always hated to walk out on a diving board that had a hemp or jute covering. There are, of course, those people who are accustomed to island living where jute and hemp are very often used as floor coverings. These people, I'm certain, don't mind their bare feet on the dried grassy rugs. I would very readily recommend jute or hemp as the floor covering in a basement family room or on outside summer porches, as neither is destroyed easily by the elements. Try durable jute and hemp rugs in the areas of a home that bear heavy traffic. Jute and hemp are available not only in the natural flaxen color, but also in pretty reds, golden yellows, blue and green tweeds, brown and black mixtures. I have myself specified woven-grass rugs for use in bedrooms, summer dining rooms, and even for living rooms.

In my very first New York home, I had a circular natural-hemp rug under my wood-top dining table. The chairs I used were lightly stained side chairs with rush seats that had belonged to my parents. The natural color of the rush on the chair seats coordinated extremely well with the natural color of the rug. Hemp and jute carpeting, wall-to-wall or in the area form, for very little achieve the look of a lot!

An Idea for Carpeting the Staircase

A friend of mine in Massachusetts found an interesting, colorful, and in-expensive way of carpeting his staircase. The staircase from my friend's first floor to his second floor consisted of 12 steps and 12 risers. The riser is that portion of the staircase noted in the illustration. For the carpeting my friend bought odd sample pieces of carpet. He paid less than one dollar for a bound carpet sample a yard long by 27 inches wide. He bought two red carpet samples, two beige carpet samples and two brown carpet samples, a total investment of less than 10 dollars including carpeting tacks. When he took the carpet samples home, he started covering his staircase. The first riser, first step, second riser and second step were covered with a red carpet sample. The next two steps and risers were covered with a beige carpet sample. For the next he used a chocolate carpet sample. For the next two,

This staircase was carpeted for less than $10.00

127

he went back to the red carpet. For the next he used beige carpet, and for the last two steps the chocolate carpet. The illustration gives an idea of the delightful effect made by this multicolored and very inexpensive stair covering. The carpet samples, by the way, need not be of the same texture.

Uinyl FLOORS ARe HeRe To STAy!

Fun with Flooring—Try Vinyl

There are many showrooms across the country that deal with vinyl flooring materials and vinyl flooring patterns. Every time I am in one of these showrooms, I feel that I am in a changing wonderland. Vinyl flooring pattern and designs are changing daily. There are beautiful solid-color vinyl materials available—bright reds, sky blues, canary yellows. There are vinyls with flecked patterns, vinyls that look like marble and travertine, vinyls that are octagonal or hexagonal in shape. There are brick vinyls in red, black, white, and gray. There is even a used-brick vinyl flooring. There is a vinyl that looks like old plank, and like the ground on the Appian way. Vinyl floors are here to stay and, to my way of thinking, they are very welcome. I find that vinyl floors are most practical and serviceable in family dining rooms and foyers. Vinyl works not only in the kitchen but in the family room as well. It can also be used on the floors of children's rooms for practicality and ease of maintenance. I have seen it used attractively in master bedrooms and family living rooms. Many patterns can be formed with vinyl. You can have a white vinyl floor with red and black feature stripping. You can have a vinyl floor with a center design and a border. You can install a brick vinyl laid in a herringbone pattern in your family kitchen. Vinyl flooring is very washable—all that is needed is warm water and a light detergent.

Chapter VII

Ways with Windows

Windows are the eyes of the home and can be treated in countless different ways: there are undercurtains, overdraperies, valances, jabots, swags, window shades, decorative filigree panels, café curtains, shutters, and jalousies. Just as there are countless colors to choose from, there are a myriad of different designs for windows. Don't think only in terms of draperies, any more than you would confine yourself to paint and/or wallpaper for walls or only wall-to-wall carpeting for floors. Examine some of the many new window ideas and try something new and daring.

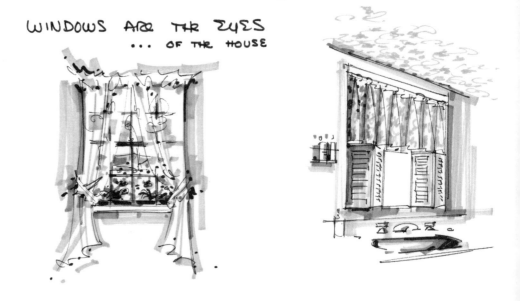

Air-conditioning and heating units can pose a big problem with window treatments. They are often located directly below the windows and project into the room some four to six inches. In such a case, draw draperies must be installed from the ceiling and on a track at least six inches from the window wall. This permits the draperies, when drawn, to clear the air-conditioning/heating unit itself. If the track is installed only two or three inches from the window wall, the drawn draperies will bulge in the center. In the summer months when the air conditioning is on, the drapery can't be drawn, as you will close out the air. In the winter, in many homes, if you draw the draperies and the heat is on, you close out the heat. One must be extremely careful to note exactly where the heating/air-conditioning units are located. In many homes where there is base-heating radiation, the convectors appear on walls other than the window wall. Study the location of your heating/air-conditioning units and consider the effect your proposed window treatment will have on your heating and/or air-conditioning system.

Valances and Overdrapery

Valances are always in good taste, and I recommend and use them often as they look well in almost every situation. The effect is a very dramatic one, especially at night, when the draperies are closed. The depth of a valance for a room with a standard 8-foot ceiling should be approximately 14 inches at its deepest point. A good way to determine the proper depth for your valance is to divide your ceiling height by 6. For example, if your living room ceiling is 12 feet high and you divide by 6, you determine that your valance should be 24 inches at its deepest point. If your ceiling height is 8 feet and you divided by 6, you would find that your valance should be 1 foot 2 inches at its deepest point. When you determine valance depth by use of the division factor 6, be certain your valance is hung from the ceiling. If you want your valance hung at the top of your window and not from your ceiling, divide your *window* height by 6. When installing a window valance and not a valance from the ceiling, the shallowest part of your valance should be at the frame of the window; therefore, your valance will actually be installed on the wall above the window. Only the deepest points in the shape of the valance will cover your window's glass portion. The illustration shows how to install valances on a wall above a window and how to install a valance from the ceiling. One of my decorating pet peeves is the valance with short pants. If a valance is hung from a ceiling, I prefer that it cover the space from the ceiling to the top of the window casing. This does not always work, however. In some instances, the distance from the top of the window can be 24 inches or 36 inches or even 49 inches. Obviously, in such cases valances are installed on the wall surfaces above the window, and valance depths should be determined from the height of the window from the floor. In most cases, valances will measure about 12 to 14 inches in depth. This is

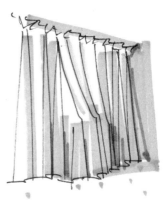

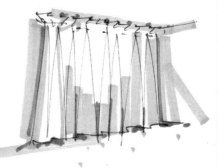

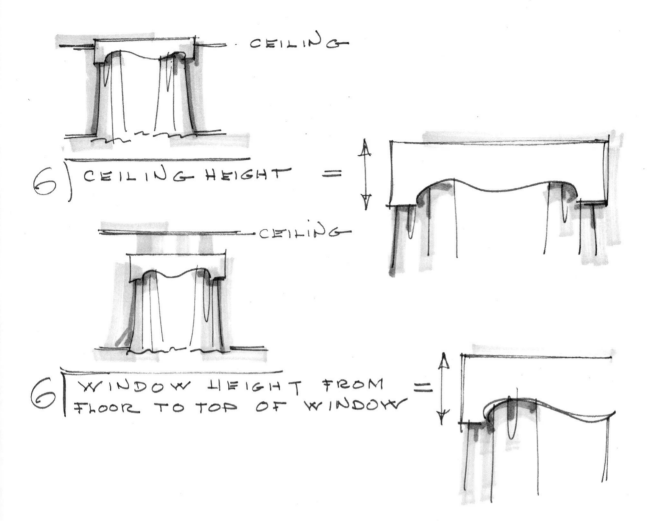

$$6\overline{)\text{CEILING HEIGHT}} = \updownarrow$$

$$6\overline{)\text{WINDOW HEIGHT FROM} \atop \text{FLOOR TO TOP OF WINDOW}} = \updownarrow$$

a general rule to which, of course, there are exceptions. But for the average single-family home, this principle will apply.

There is some question as to how valances should be made. Should fabric be applied to a plywood cutout or should valance fabric be backed and stitched to buckram? Each method has its own merits. The plywood valance to which the fabric has been applied must be completely removed each time it is cleaned. The buckram valance is more easily removed for cleaning. Sometimes, physical conditions influence the way valances are made. I recall one made for one of my apartment-decorating assignments. It was of cutout plywood some 18 feet long and when it came to installing it there was no way to get the 18-foot valance into the apartment house elevator. It had to be hoisted from the street, as did the 10-foot sofa, and at considerable expense. Had it been made in two sections, it would have had a center seam, which my client did not want. Had it been made in three sections, there would have been two side seams. Of course, the plywood valance in sections could have been assembled on the job and then covered with fabric after it was in place. On my decorating jobs where long valances are required, I now always use buckram.

Buckram, like crinoline, is a stiff material that gives substance and permanence to fabric. With buckram, one does not have to worry that the valance will sag or fall out of place. Buckram keeps the fabric evenly stretched and taut.

On Café Curtains

Café curtains are very popular in home decorating. I think the word "café" has something to do with this popularity. Indeed, curtains hung on rods were first used in the bistro or café; thus we get the words "café curtains." I like café curtains hung in the family kitchen or in a study or in a boy's room. Yet, to say that they are limited to these rooms in the home would

135

be a mistake. Café curtains are very often used today, and most effectively, in almost every room of the home—at the windows in the living room/dining room combination and even at the windows in the master bedroom. Recently, for the dining room of a Southern California home, I hung a wall of café curtains on one pole, from ceiling to floor. The pole and rings were painted a bright lime green, the same lime green being used as the color for fringes on the bottom of the curtains. The curtains themselves were of a nubby beige linen. Inasmuch I believe that windows are the eyes of the home, the curtaining was lined with a lime green and white striped cotton. The curtains were as delightful from the outside as they were from the inside.

Hanging Café Curtains in Two Tiers

A café curtain can be hung in one, two, or even three tiers. I would not recommend hanging café curtaining in any more than three tiers unless your ceilings are extremely high and you have a giant movable ladder at hand every time you want to open or close the upper tier. The café curtain hung in two tiers is the most common manner of installing this type of window treatment.

For the windows in Junior's room, why not try upper and lower café curtains? Inexpensive, ready-made café curtains are available in the drapery department of your local department store, along with adjustable rods. The brass rods simply snap into the window casing. The advantages of the upper and lower café are many. The lower café curtain can be closed for privacy and the upper curtain open for light. When the outside sunlight is strong, the top tier of cafés can be closed and the lower tier left opened.

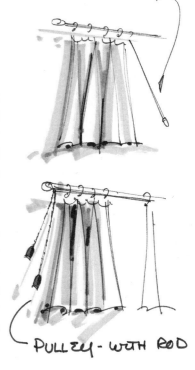

BATON

PULLEY - WITH ROD

Café curtains can be installed on rods with rings that are closed or opened simply by hand. In other cases, café curtains can be installed with draw pulley attachments. Café curtains can also be installed with "baton pulls," as illustrated in the drawing.

Louver Shutters, Alone and with Cafés

Louver shutters are effective decorations for the eyes of the home, appealing from the outside as well as from the inside. If your home has a third or fourth bedroom that is not occupied by one of the children, why not turn it into a combination den and guest room, using louver shutters at the windows?

In the illustration, you will see the study/guest room. At the windows, louver shutters have been hung in two tiers. The bottom tier can be closed for privacy and the top tier left open for light. One of the advantages of louver shutters is the fact that both tiers can be closed and the shutter panels adjusted so that light can come through. Louver shutter panels can be adjusted to direct light up or down. Those shown in the illustration have a walnut stain. Louver shutters are also most effective in a painted finish. Try sparkling pink louver shutters at the windows in your daughter's room or try bright red louver shutters in your family kitchen, or perhaps a row of sunny lemon louvers would brighten the windows in your living room/ dining room.

Louver shutters with café curtains are frequently used in home decorating. The louvers and cafés are installed within the window casing. The louvers can be installed on the top and the cafés on the lower portion of the window, or vice versa, as you prefer. The illustration shows louver shutters at a kitchen window above a cabinet sink unit. The louvers have been painted sunny yellow, the same color as the counter tops. The curtains are of a fabric that matches the wallpaper used on the kitchen ceiling. The louvers were installed at the lower portion of the window for practical reasons. Water splashing against the lacquered wood louvers will do little or no damage. Had the curtains and louvers been reversed, the curtaining would have been destroyed in little or no time.

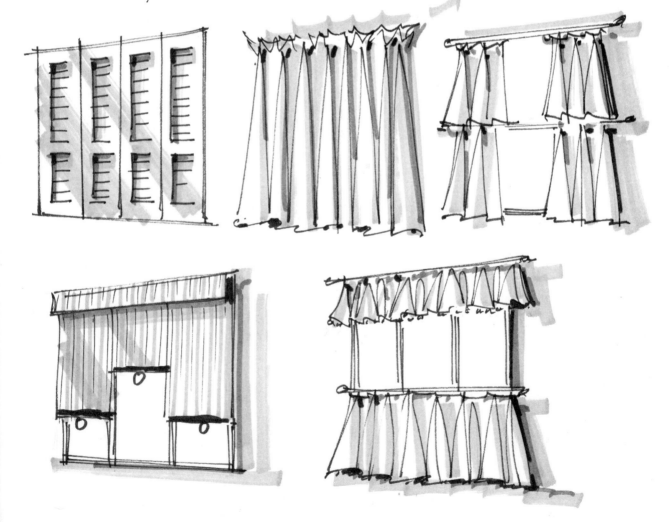

Lower Louvers with a Swag Valance

For an upper New York State home, I used in the dining room a window treatment featuring a swag valance with jabots hung above a louver shutter treatment. The louvers were painted spanking white and the valance swag and jabots were made of bright green fabric and were lined with a yellow and white flower print. Such a treatment requires a window shade to be installed at the top portion of the window, which, when pulled, comes to the top portion of the louver shutters.

A Paper Valance for Baby's Room

A young couple I know used one of my favorite and often suggested paper-valance treatments for the windows in their baby's room. The valance is made using colored construction paper that has been accordion-folded and punched with holes. The window rod simply slides through the punched holes of the paper. In the illustration, you can see the accordion valance. The valance can be made of one-color paper, perhaps sky blue or lemon for a boy or shell pink or red for a girl. In the case of my young friend, she made her valance candy cane or peppermint stick in effect, using alternating colors of white, pink, and red. The paper was 9 inches by 12 inches in size. First, she placed three folded sheets of white paper on the rod, then three sheets of pink paper, then three sheets of red. The alternating system was used until the rod was completely filled. Be careful not to fit the folded sheets tightly together on the rod. Allow them to expand as an open accordion. Your valance should look like the accordion when open and full, not like the accordion when closed. A white opaque window shade is installed in the windowcasing, behind the accordion paper valance.

YOUR LOCAL DEPARTMENT STORE
— CURTAIN SHOP —

On Glass Curtains

Today glass curtains are used very often. There are glass curtains available in most every curtain shop in the country as well as at the drapery department in your local department store. You can find glass curtains ready-made that will fit your window sizes. When purchasing ready-made curtains, either of glass or of a cotton fiber or of some other fiber, be certain you have a note of your window sizes. Bring to your drapery man or to the salesman in the curtain section of your local department store full information. Mark down the width of your windows from casing to casing; you must also know the height of your windows from casing to casing. You must note the measurement from your window sills to the floor, and you should note the measurement from the top of your windows to the ceiling. Your curtain man can help you most fruitfully only if he knows your exact window measurements.

I particularly recommend glass curtains for practical and long-lasting reasons. In almost every color you can think of, they can easily be washed in your own washing machine and rehung in a day. There are even glass curtains that do not require ironing. Many are the young housewives who rave about glass curtains because of their durability and long-lasting value.

Don't Hang Yourself with Overhangings

Many a mistake is made in home decorating when the young wife is sold a bill of goods on overhangings. By overhangings I mean too much curtaining at the windows of a small room. In the illustration you can see the windows of a living room that are overhung with fabric. Overhanging tends to reduce the size of rooms, close out needed air and light, and in general give rooms a stuffy, claustrophobic feeling. Windows in small rooms should be treated with the light approach. This simply means that you should hang a draw drapery of a transparent fabric or of a fabric that matches your wall color. If your walls are white and your room is small, use white draw draperies to unify space and to give the illusion that your room is larger than it actually is. Never should windows in small rooms be cascaded with swags of heavy fabric or patterned draw draperies.

The illustration shows three window treatments for small rooms. The first is simply a draw drapery made from white transparent nylon or dacron or glass curtaining. The second combines transparent sheer undercurtains with a window valance. The third combines side-trellis screen panels with a white draw drapery. I have used the side-trellis screen panels on a number of home-decorating projects, and the screens have always met with great success. The trellis can be painted a sparkling color to coordinate with a room's decor, perhaps royal blue, persimmon, or gold. Or line the back of a white-painted trellis with a colorful plain fabric. Visualize for a moment a living room with an emerald-green carpet, white walls, and white draw curtains. At each side of the window at the end of the living room stand two trellis folding-screen panels. The white trelliswork stands out against a background of emerald-green cotton fabric. Trellis folding panels need not be lined with fabric that is stretched and tacked to the frame of each panel. One might fill the back of the trellis panel with a colored paper or with painted plywood.

THE LIGHT APPROACH

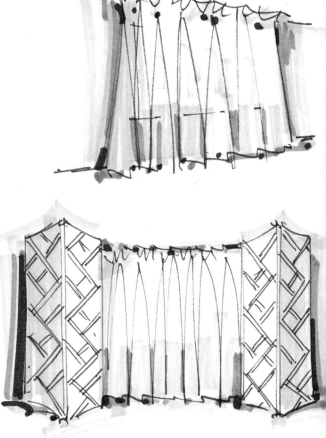

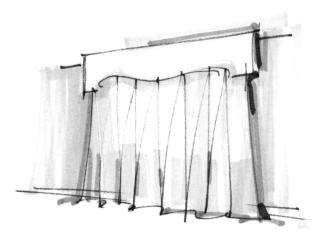

On Window Shades

Window shades have made and are still making strong inroads on the decorating scene. Not so many years ago, one thought of shades as those green paper rollers that, on occasion, came loose from the windows or refused to roll up. Window shades have grown up since those days. Rarely today does one even see a green shade, unless it is made of fabric or a coated

DON'T HANG YOURSELF WITH......
OUER HANGINGS!

TRY THIS INSTEAD!

vinyl material. Green paper shades were used because they closed out light. Today, opaque shades made of any color, including white, can do the job. White opaque shades close out as much light as do green shades.

Basically, there are three kinds of shades: the roller shade, sometimes decorated, sometimes plain; the Roman shade; and the Austrian shade. The Roman shade is pulled by the cord method and folds up in layers or tiers. The Austrian shade is likewise pulled by cord and rises up in graceful puffs. Roman shades that fold up in layers can be made of fabric and can also be made of a combination of yarns and wood materials. Some people refer to this type of wood and yarn Roman shade as the "matchstick shade." These

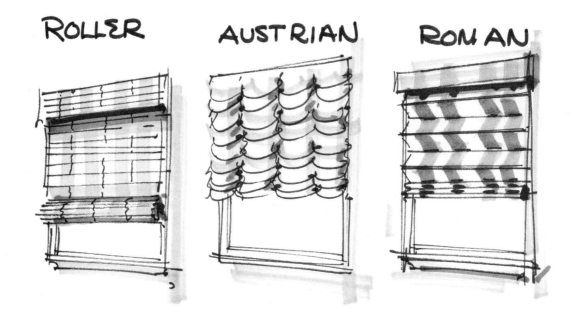

ROLLER   AUSTRIAN   ROMAN

are actually slats of wood, sometimes bamboo, laid horizontally and connected one to the other by colored yarns. In my own office, I have matchstick shades hung at all windows, with the sticks alternately black and white and connected by white yarn. Matchstick shades need not be only Roman in style, that is, operated by a pull cord. They are also available in roller form.

On the Austrians

Austrian shades seem to represent formality. They are often seen, with ruchings and fringes and tassels, hung at the windows of fancy restaurants and in elegantly decorated ballrooms. Austrian shades can be and often are used by the homemaker at the windows in the master bedroom or at the window in the guest powder room or hall bathroom. Austrian shades, or puff shades, as they are called by some, or festoon blinds, as the English call them, can be purchased as ready-mades in the curtain department of your local department store or curtain shop. In the illustrations, I have shown an Austrian-shade treatment in a master bedroom and in a dining

MATCHSTICK SHADES

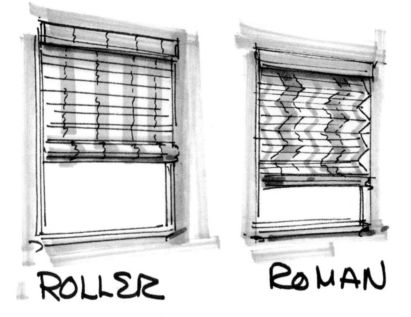

ROLLER   ROMAN

room. While the Austrian shade is graceful, I do not feel that it is the most practical window treatment in the family home. To look their best, they must be always sparkling white, always dusted carefully, and always hung in full folds. True, there are puff shades made of colorful prints and dark-colored fabrics. Shades using these special fabrics are generally custom-made, however. If finances permit, I recommend puff shades of a colorful cotton spring-flower chintz for Sis's room or for the master bedroom. Austrian shades are never right for Junior's room or for Dad's study or for the family living room. If your home is one of those old single-family dwellings with high ceilings and high French windows, however, you might consider Austrian curtains for the living room. I do hope you won't have the job, however, of washing or ironing the puffs!

Decorating Your Own Roller Window Shades

Those handy with a stencil can create their own designs on window shades. One friend of mine stenciled blue stars on the window shades in her fourteen-year-old son's room. After stenciling the stars, she painted a 3-inch red horizontal stripe on the bottom part of the shade. The shades were most effective in a white-painted room that was decorated with a royal-blue cotton rug and a bright red corduroy fitted spread on her son's 3-foot 3-inch twin bed.

If you don't feel confident with a stencil (and I don't know why—it's so easy), try putting a border of contact paper on your window shades. I know one homemaker who completely covered the interior side of her bedroom roller shades with a pink and melon plaid contact paper. She used the same contact paper on her bed wall in the bedroom, on the walls and ceiling in the bathroom, and even on her wastebasket, tissue-holder box and toothbrush glass.

On Decorative Screens and Beads

We can't leave our discussion of window treatments without talking about decorative screens and beads. Decorative screens have come up in the ranks in home planning. I often use sliding decorative screens as the window treatments in home living rooms or dining rooms and screen panels as the window treatments in bedrooms, for those with a bent for Oriental, modern, and low decor.

There are many types of screens that can be used in home decorating. There are Oriental Shoji screens. There are filigree screens in all types of wood cutout designs. There are wrought-iron screens. There are plexiglass screens. There are wood and fabric screens.

Next time you visit your local carpentry shop, hardware store, or lumber yard, ask the owner to show you a catalogue of precut, unfinished screen designs. Tell him you're interested in filigree screens that you can install on a ceiling track in front of the windows in your dining room or living room.

I'm certain your local hardware store, carpentry shop, or lumber yard will have information about decorative screens, their sizes, and their manner of installation. In my first New York City apartment, I installed decorative screens at the windows simply by following the directions given me by the screen manufacturer in his brochure.

On Spools and Beads

Beaded window curtains and door curtains are not new! While beaded doorways and beaded window curtains were seen often in movies of the 1930s and 1940s, they were rarely if ever found in the home. Today, however, beaded curtains are the rage. Plastic and glass threaded-bead curtaining can be used in your living room and also very effectively used in your dining room. Bead curtains can be installed on a traverse rod and can be opened and closed with the simple pull of the end.

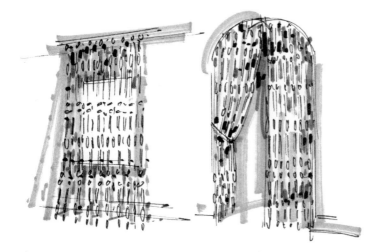

For the window design in a fifteen-year-old girl's bedroom, the girl herself created a draw drapery of red and pink spools. The spools were wooden thread spools, many of which she had collected herself by canvassing her neighbors and friends. Her father later told me that he had helped the cause himself by buying some 300 wooden spools for his daughter from a thread company. He added, however, that the spools were most inexpensive. The young lady spray-painted one half the spools pink and one half the spools vibrant red before stringing them onto 8-foot lengths of strong white string. At the top of each 8-foot length of string, she tied a loop which was connected and hung from a carrier on her traverse rod. At the bottom of each 8-foot length of string, she tied a strong knot before commencing her spool-threading activity. I have seen this window treatment and I find it creative, exciting, and effective from a decorating point of view. During the day, the light filters through the spool-beaded curtain. At night, she draws her white opaque window shade, which sets a beautiful backdrop for her great window design.

Chapter VIII

Furniture: How To Select, What To Select, When To Buy

There are many people today who, when discussing furniture and furnishings, feel that they must be knowledgeable on all the periods and styles, that they must be able to distinguish a Louis XIV from a Louis XV chair. The study of furniture design and style is a long and involved process and I admire those of my friends who have a good working knowledge of furniture styles. There are many books that go deeply into the study of furniture, and to locate such books I suggest a visit to your local library and a talk with the head librarian. The following pages show sketches of 27 furniture styles that are the basis for many of the furniture lines being created and marketed today.

They include the following:

1. Egyptian (4000 B.C.–300 A.D.)
2. Grecian (1200 B.C.–300 B.C.)
3. Roman (600 B.C.–400 A.D.)
4. Gothic (1100–1500)
5. Italian Renaissance (1443–1564)
6. Flemish Renaissance (1500–1600)
7. Spanish Renaissance (1500–1650)
8. Tudor—Elizabethan (1509–1603)
9. French Renaissance (1515–1643)
10. Chinese (1600–1700)
11. Jacobean (1603–1688)
12. French Provincial (1610–1800)
13. Early American
    Before the Revolution, British influenced (1620–1795)
    After the Revolution, French influenced (1795–1847)
14. Louis XIV (1643–1715)
15. William and Mary (1689–1702)

16. Queen Anne (1702–1714)

17. Georgian (1714–1820)

18. Chippendale (1705–1779)

19. Louis XV (1715–1774)

20. Sheraton (1750–1806)

21. Adam (1765–1790)

22. Hepplewhite (1770–1790)

23. Louis XVI (1774–1793)

24. Duncan Phyfe (1795–1854)

25. Directoire (1795–1804)

26. Empire (1799–1814)

27. Victorian (1837–1901)

After looking at the drawings, you will hopefully be able to identify what period was in the furniture manufacturer's mind when he created your dining chair or bedroom night table. If you can't identify the style, don't fret. When furniture manufacturers put a new line on the market today, they may disregard the authentic details of a style and create furniture details of their own.

There are today, however, many furniture designs that do not take their basis from any of the styles presented. I have always been one for growth and change and have always felt that period and contemporary modern furniture can be combined, provided it is done with an eye on scale and composition. I like to see a stainless-steel-based glass-top coffee table in a French parlor. In my own home, I combine what I like of the new with what I respect and like of the old. I firmly believe that the family home should reflect the personalities of all members of the family. Louis XIV was not afraid to project his personality in the furnishing and decoration of his country palace at Versailles. A family home should be furnished around the personal needs, likes, dislikes, wishes, and ambitions of the family members, not around a style that is currently in vogue or around a style your neighbor has in her home. I have no objection to your buying the same sofa as your neighbor, provided you honestly like it and find it comfortable. Do not buy furniture simply to keep up with the neighbors' tastes. Buy furniture and furnishings that you yourself like and enjoy.

Buying Furniture with a Budget in Mind

Rome wasn't built in a day, nor was a home decorated and furnished

EGYPTIAN
(4000 BC — 300 AD)

GRECIAN
(1200 - 300 BC)

ROMAN
(600 BC - 400 AD)

GOTHIC
(1100 - 1500)

ITALIAN RENAISSANCE
(1443-1564)

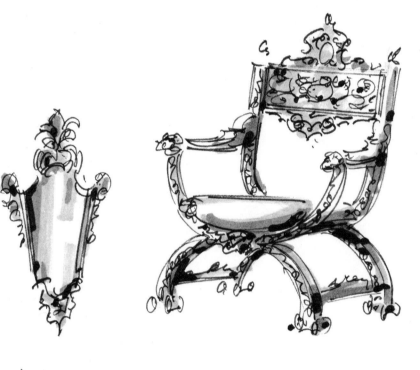

FLEMISH RENAISSANCE
(1500 – 1600)

SPANISH RENAISSANCE
(1500 – 1650)

TUDOR- ELIZABETHAN
(1509 - 1603)

FRENCH RENAISSANCE
(1515 - 1643)

CHINESE
(1600 – 1700)

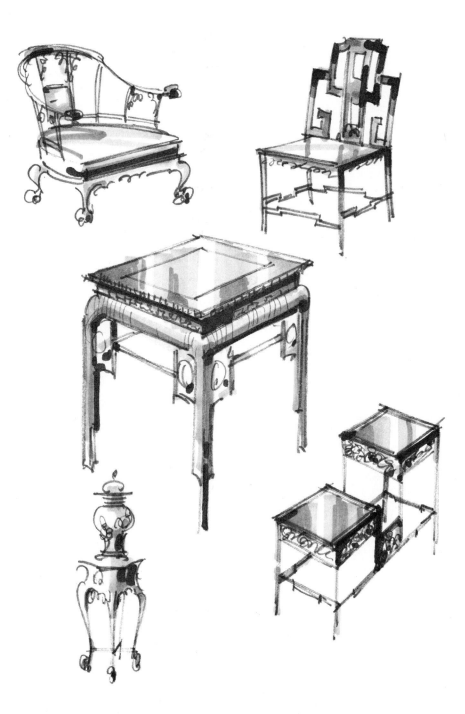

JACOBEAN
(1603 – 1688)

FRENCH PROVINCIAL
(1610 - 1800)

EARLY AMERICAN
– BRITISH INFLUENCE
(1620–1795)

EARLY AMERICAN
– FRENCH INFLUENCE (1795–1847)

LOUIS XIV
(1643 - 1715)

WILLIAM & MARY
(1689 - 1702)

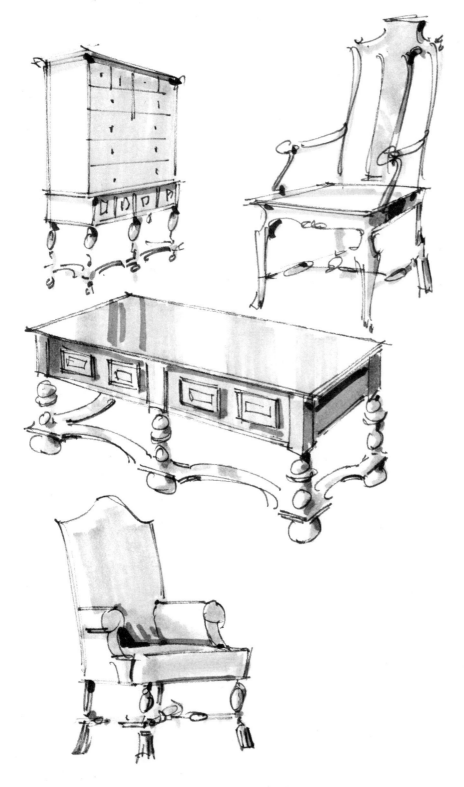

QUEEN ANNE
(1702-1714)

GEORGIAN
(1714 - 1820)

CHIPPENDALE
(1705-1779)

LOUIS XV
(1715-1774)

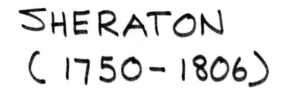

SHERATON
(1750-1806)

ADAM
(1765-1790)

HEPPLEWHITE
(1770 - 1790)

LOUIS XVI
(1774-1793)

DUNCAN-PHYFE
(1795-1854)

DIRECTOIRE
(1795–1804)

EMPIRE
(1799-1814)

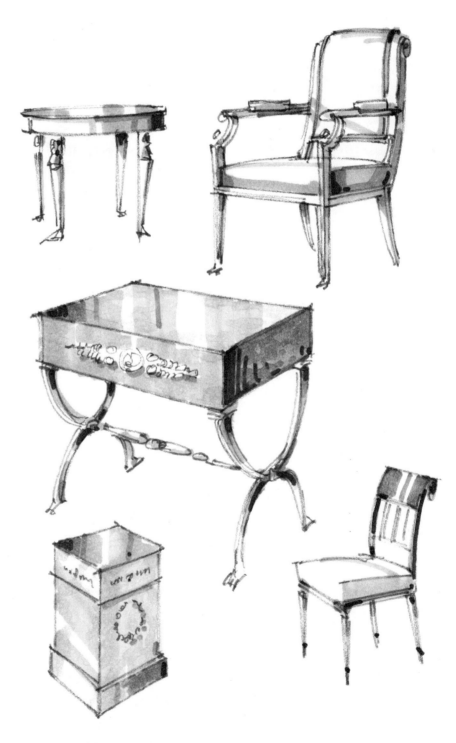

VICTORIAN

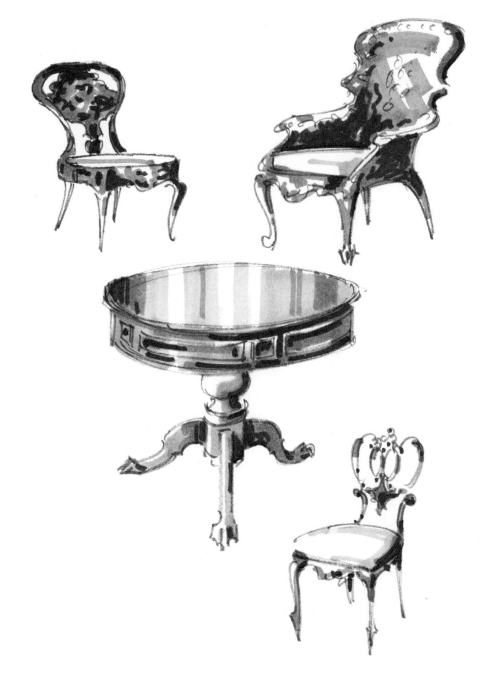

overnight. You don't have to decorate and furnish your home with all new pieces straight off the floor of the nearest decorating shop. Before buying furniture for the home, make a careful study of what you have in relation to what you need. Will the sofa do for the time being, allowing money to be spent for that needed dining table? Will the old headboards do in the twins' bedroom, perhaps with a fresh coat of pink paint? If those headboards can be used, you can use the money for a new wing chair to set by the fireplace. Can the old carpeting be used by cutting it into an area rug and using it in the dining area? A young, on-the-rise couple with a family should be budget conscious. Money should be spent wisely, perhaps for new bedspreads and curtains in the master bedroom, perhaps for a good-looking striped wallpaper for the bedroom hallway, perhaps for a new pair of living room club chairs or a new lamp to use on the bedroom night table or a crystal chandelier to hang over the dining room table.

For those just starting out in the furniture-buying department, furniture can be purchased in the following order:

Time-Buying Guide

for Couples with Absolutely No Furniture

1. Bed (a 4-foot-6-inch or a 6-foot-6-inch-wide double).
2. Night table, dresser, high chest. NOTE: Night table, dresser, and high chest do not necessarily have to match.
3. Mirror to hang above bedroom dresser.
4. A bedroom lamp for night table and one for dresser.
5. Kitchen table, chairs for kitchen table.
6. Living room sofa.
7. Living room plywood-top end table—30-inch diameter.
   NOTE: Have a felt circle cut and drape over the plywood-top table to the floor.
8. Lamp for living room end table.
9. Coffee table (for living room).
10. Club chairs (preferably matching).
11. Built-in unit to accommodate new stereo and wedding-present television set. NOTE: Built-in unit should have a place for bookshelves.
12. Bedroom lounge chair and ottoman.
13. Dining table and chairs. NOTE: Use family-room dining table until you get to purchase #15.

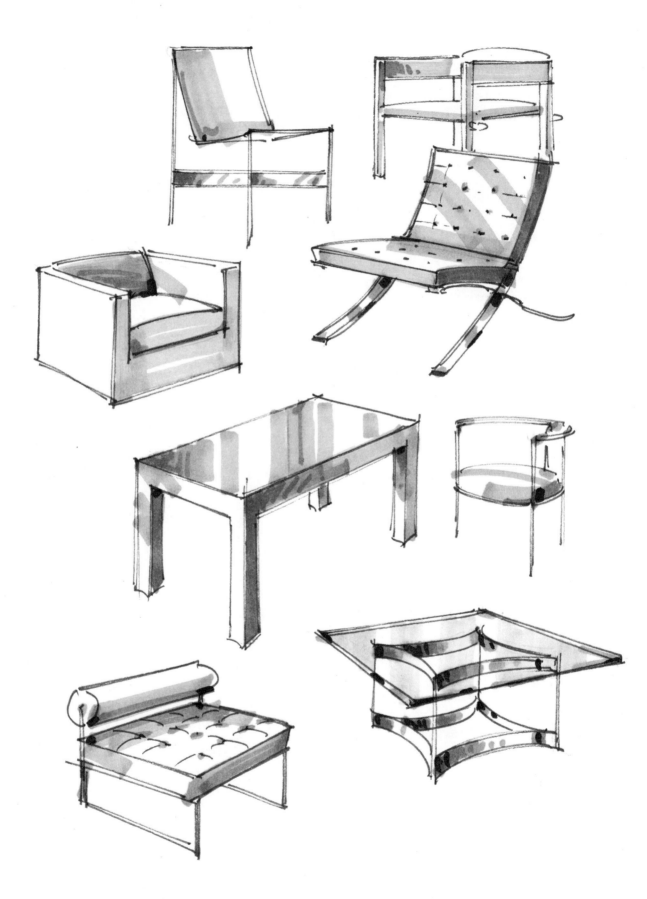

14. Second end table. NOTE: Perhaps you'll find some interesting antique trunk or low chest that would accommodate your needs.
15. Lamp for second end table. NOTE: Until purchase #15, you have used one lamp on a round table and the overhead light in the living room. You may also have used an old standing lamp that Mother gave you.
16. Dining area serving buffet.
17. Chandelier to hang over dining table to replace the inexpensive globe fixture that came with the house.
18. Console table for foyer.
19. Mirror to hang over foyer console table.
20. Occasional chairs to pull up to coffee table or to set left and right of television/built-in cabinet stereo unit.

The young couple will buy in the order presented only in the case where money keeps coming rather than babies. If baby arrives before your purchase of the living room coffee table, substitute a crib for the table, a bassinette for club chairs, and the doctor bills for the built-in unit. Don't fret, however; the time will come when you can go back to your buying list and check off additional numbers. An old friend once told me: "As long as there is thought, there is change—and change always brings additional buying." I believe this. Indeed I have never known anyone who could say, "I'm through with buying furniture."

Can You Refinish an Old Painted Piece?

Removing the paint from an old piece of furniture is not so difficult as it might appear. A young single friend of mine had in her home an old, interesting secretary desk that had been painted black and which she wanted to paint a bright Chinese red. She found an old paint brush and a pair of gloves and began applying the paint remover to the secretary. After the paint remover had been applied to an area on the desk, the old black paint was removed with a scraper. Some people use a #3-grade steel wool, rather than a scraper, to remove the old paint.

For areas of the piece that had ornate carvings, the old paint was removed with a toothbrush and a nut pick—of course, after the paint remover had been applied. When the desk was down to its original stained state, my friend waited a day or two, then gave the piece a fresh and striking coat of Chinese-red paint. The Chinese-red color coordinated beautifully with her apple-green wall-to-wall carpeting, her apple-green-on-white bamboo-design chintz drapery and her Chinese-red patent-vinyl lounge chairs.

On Removing the Stain from a Table

A friend of mine from Oregon gave me this tip and I pass it on to you. To remove the stain from a piece of furniture, simply use a good bleach. The bleach can be used full strength or it can be diluted—one-half bleach and one-half water. Apply the bleach to a piece of furniture outside your home, not inside. Use it with care. Bleach can do to wood what it does to clothes.

To Create a Satin Look

An old-fashioned New England formula for creating a satin look on furniture is to rub the stained piece with a solution of equal parts of white vinegar, boiled linseed oil, and turpentine. Mix the parts of the solution in a jar or container and shake well. Rub the solution onto the piece you are bringing into the realm of the special beautiful furniture. Let the solution soak on the piece for ten minutes. Rub off the excess solution and let dry. Wait 24 hours before applying the second treatment. After 24 hours have passed, again apply the white vinegar, boiled linseed oil, and turpentine solution. Let the solution again soak into the piece some ten minutes, then rub off excess. The secrets of a good satin finish are two:

1. Let the solution soak only ten minutes.
2. Apply the solution daily. It may take 20 applications for you to get the desired satin finish you wish.

On End Tables and Coffee Tables

End tables beside a sofa need not match; in fact, I prefer that they don't! Nor does the balanced room need two matching end tables, two matching lounge chairs, two matching end-table lamps, two matching pillows on the sofa, and two matching coffee tables in front of the sofa. In the sketch, I have illustrated the matching room. Many people (and decorators) follow

the matching balance theory. The theory may work, but I personally feel that the result is much too contrived, planned, and dull.

The second illustration shows a sofa grouping that is balanced and yet is not matching. At one end of the sofa is a square captain's chest of drawers. At the other end of the sofa is a round table. The lounge chairs used sit together in front of the windows and beside the captain's chest. The normal placement for lounge chairs is to the right and left, respectively, of the sofa, beside the end tables.

The Railroad Look

Study the illustration marked "The Railroad Look." You will see the long 7-foot sofa has been flanked by two rectangular end tables. The coffee table is also rectangular. The picture hung above the sofa is a long horizontal picture. The effect presented is strictly "railroad." Everything runs on a track in one direction.

When planning a grouping, stay away from the railroad look. If you have a bent for matching end tables, use round end tables beside a long sofa. End tables should generally be the height of your sofa arms. An inch or two higher or lower, however, is really not a critical error.

On Cocktail and Coffee Tables

One of my pet peeves in home furnishing is little coffee tables. I dislike them because there is hardly room on their surface for a glass and napkin to say nothing of an ashtray, a cigarette container, a plate of hors d'oeuvres, a bowl of flowers, or a magazine or two.

When considering the purchase of a coffee or cocktail table, get one that is large enough for a tea service, a bowl of flowers, an ashtray, etc. I think you'll enjoy the large coffee table, as will your guests who come for coffee or cocktails. If your sofa is about 8 feet long, choose a rectangular coffee table, some 5 feet long by 26 inches wide. If you prefer a round cocktail table, think of one 30 inches in diameter or larger, if your room can take it. About coffee table height: the table should be lower than the height of your sofa seat, in order not to break the line of the sofa.

The living rooms in single-family homes are often small when it comes to entertaining large groups at a buffet or cocktail party. For families who entertain a lot, I suggest a nesting end-table grouping or a set of pull-out tables under the cocktail table. There are also many inexpensive sets of folding cocktail or serving tables available on the market.

On Upholstered and Occasional Chairs

Decorating should never follow an exact plan. Too often, designers have given formulas for decorating. One will say that the lounge chairs should match; another proclaims the doctrine that every sofa should be flanked by two upholstered matching chairs, two matching end tables, and two matching lamps. No two of my decorating projects have the same look and personality. Formula decorating does work, but it's not for me, and I hope it's not for you.

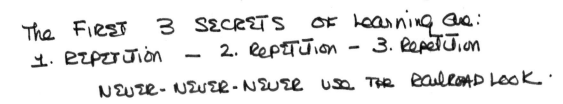

THE FIRST 3 SECRETS OF Learning are:
1. REPETITION — 2. REPETITION — 3. REPETITION
NEVER-NEVER-NEVER USE THE RAILROAD LOOK.

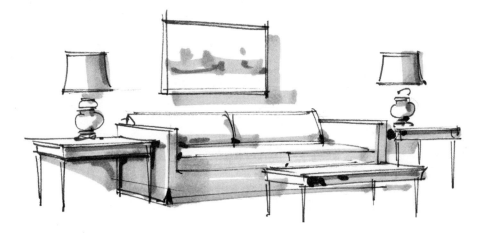

Lounge chairs can be purchased in pairs if you like, but they do not always have to be placed to the left and right of the sofa. The illustration shows three ways to use matching lounge chairs in a sofa grouping.

Occasional chairs generally combine wood with upholstery. Wing chairs, cane-backed barrel chairs, bamboo chairs with pad seats, deck chairs, French oval-back chairs are all occasional chairs. (See illustration.)

Occasional chairs can be used in pairs. I once designed and decorated a Georgian-like living room using a pair of occasional wing chairs at the left and right of the fireplace. The chairs were covered in a lemon and white striped fabric. The wing chair, because of its high back, gives balance to a

room. Think of how your living room would look if all the furniture were on one wall. Rooms need balance! If you use a high breakfront on one wall in your living room, the opposite wall should have a balancing furniture arrangement, such as a sofa with a large picture hanging above.

Occasional chairs are effective when used as pull-ups in a conversation grouping. These chairs are used only when you have more guests than you have lounge seating. Your lounge seating includes your fully upholstered sofa and club chairs. You can have lounge chairs also that have some wood showing on the arms and back, as well as wood legs. If you like slipcovers, better buy fully upholstered lounge chairs, as lounge chairs with wood arms are difficult to slipcover!

The occasional chair in a conversation grouping can be used alone. Occasional chairs can also be purchased in pairs or they can be purchased in triplets or quintuplets, depending on your need. The occasional chairs to be used in a conversation grouping are not the barrel-back caned-arm chairs, nor are they the wing chairs. The occasional chair for the sofa grouping is light and open in effect: for example, the open-back bamboo chair or the French oval-back armchair.

One of My Favorites

Call them what you like—deck chairs, director's chairs, safari chairs—they are all the same to me. They can be used at a card-table grouping, at a desk, around the dining table, or as the occasional chairs at a sofa grouping. Indeed, the deck chair is a standard design that can coordinate with many kinds of decor. Deck chairs can be purchased in a folding form and easily stored away until the time they are needed. Safari chairs also are

THE DECK CHAIR!
THE DIRECTOR'S CHAIR!
THE SAFARI CHAIR!

made in nonfoldable form. In such cases where the chair does not fold, its covering or upholstery can be anything from fabric to fur to naugahyde. A Chicago furniture firm makes a delightful nonfoldable safari chair that sells for very little and which I have used for a dramatic and comfortable effect in many home decorating jobs. Folding deck chairs can be purchased at nominal amounts; these deck chairs have canvas seats and backs. The canvas seats come in a range of colors from apple green to white to royal blue to black to red. They are also available in a number of different wood finishes—white, natural, black, green, navy blue, and lemon. When looking for an inexpensive, good-looking occasional chair, consider the deck, director, or safari chair.

FURNITURE FOR THE OUT-OF-DOORS

Chapter IX

Looking at Light: Adding with Accessories

God gave us natural light, but for only a certain number of hours a day. In the spring and summer, we have that light for more hours than we do in the fall and winter. Study your light source before buying or building a house. The kitchen, in order for it to have maximum daylight, should face east or south. If a terrace is built, it should face east so that mornings it will be sunny and bright, and shady and cool in the afternoons. Studying light source is also of great importance when selecting fabrics for curtains and treatments for windows. If the master bedroom faces west, the morning sun will not be a factor, but the room will receive the full value of the afternoon sun, a sun that is not so warm or penetrating as that in the morning. The windows in the master bedroom, therefore, can be covered with a sheer fabric that filters the afternoon sunlight. Should the master bedroom face east, the curtaining used on the windows would have to be strong and of a good fiber, first, to block the early morning sun and second, because intense sun can fade fabric colors, particularly those in the blue family, and can rot fabrics very quickly. I recall an experience I had while decorating a charming single-family home in Pennsylvania. For the living room the owners had selected a white-on-white sheer vertical-striped fabric for undercurtains. I believe the fabric was one of those composition fabrics of silk and rayon. The curtains were hung at windows that received the morning sun, and intense morning sun at that! In less than six months, the undercurtains were literally in shreds. This would not have occurred had my client used a glass undercurtain or undercurtains made of heavy linen casement material.

On Candles

The candle is one of the most pleasant, delightful, decorative, and utilitarian accessory items used in the home. Consider for a moment a fall supper-party table set with a golden-colored table cloth, chocolate placemats, and rich orange napkins. The flowers in the center of the table are golden and white chrysanthemums. The candles used in single candlesticks to the left and right of the centerpiece are copper-colored.

I cannot overemphasize the importance of candlelight dining. Candles are relatively inexpensive and should be used often! Start using candlelight at all the family evening meals and I guarantee it won't be long before you find that a dinner table without candlelight has no glow!

ACCESSORIES FOR THE HOME

THE Candle IS one of my favorite accessories!

On Candle Sconces

Candle sconces are a great wall decoration and there are a number of different styles of candle brackets available. There are wrought-iron sconces that look beautiful on white walls with Spanish-style wood furnishings. There are brass wall candle sconces with hurricane globes that look well

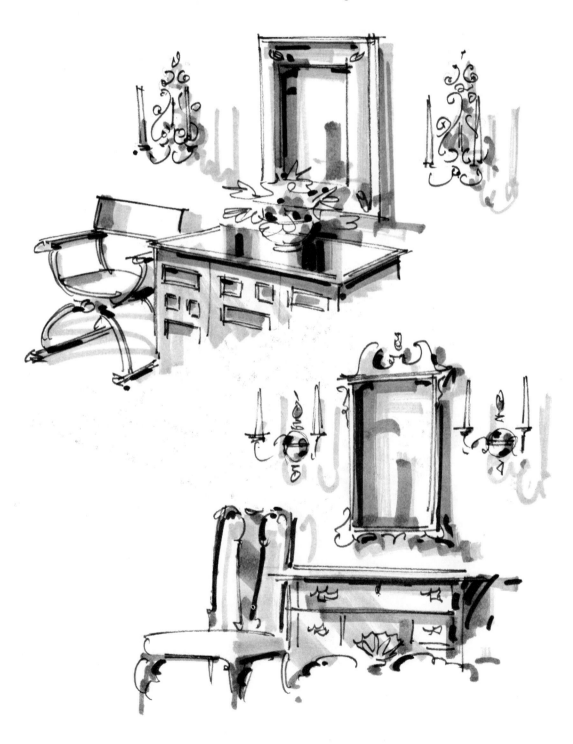

in period as well as in modern settings. There are wood Colonial candle wall sconces that can bring some real country charm into your home. The illustration shows a number of types of candle sconces you might consider for the dining room, living room, or foyer.

While dining in the home of a young New York couple, my eye was caught by a pair of candlesticks on the buffet table. When I inquired about them, my friend explained to me that the candlesticks were part of an old wood balustrade. What I thought to be actual antique candlesticks were simply turned-wood uprights from an old staircase. In the illustration, I have shown the buffet setting in my friend's home. The candles used on top of the balustrade turnings were large, thick-diameter church candles that had been melted on the bottoms and stuck to the tops of the turnings. I can visualize such candlesticks not only in a stained-wood finish, but also in colors—perhaps sage green, melon, poinsettia red, and spicy mustard.

One of the most welcoming touches to your home can be a pair of candlelit wall sconces hung to the left and right of a console table mirror in the foyer. If you use candle sconces in your home, or if you plan to use candles for dining-table decorations, be certain to buy dripless candles. Candle wax can damage wood tabletops and can mess up your table cloth. If you have to use candles that drip, be certain that you have a plastic bobêche around the base of each candle to catch the dripping wax.

Another word of advice: Buy candles that are smokeless as well as dripless. Candle smoke can discolor your walls and ceilings quicker than you can imagine.

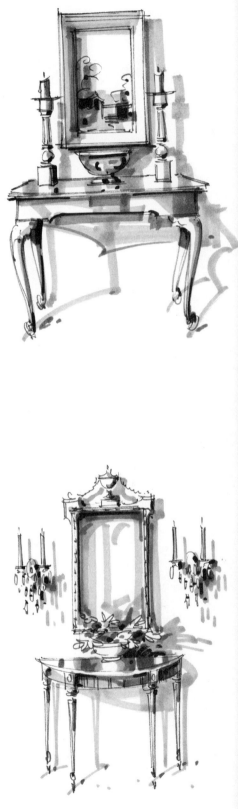

Man Discovers Electricity

The minute I begin discussing electrical outlets and wiring with one of my clients, I see his face drop and his eyes take on a blank stare. Electrical wiring and outlet arrangements always seem to put people into a state of bewilderment, possibly because one never understands where electricity comes from and how it gets to the plug on the living room wall. For our purposes, however, you only have to be certain that every room in your home has enough outlets. Remember, there will be times when the vacuum cleaner has to be operated. There will be times you'll want and need an outlet in your foyer. A basic working knowledge of electricity is invaluable. Buy a simple manual on electricity, one that goes into some detail about wiring, outlets, how properly to hang ceiling fixtures, how to splice a lamp cord and attach a plug. When planning a furniture layout for any room in your home, hopefully with your scaled furniture cutouts, make sure your living room end tables or bedroom night tables fall in a place where there are wall plugs, as you will be placing lamps on your tables. If, in your living room layout plan, you find that your end tables and desk fall at spots where there are no outlets, discuss the matter with an electrician who can arrange to have additional outlets installed in the walls for you. Ask for his estimate of costs before you give him the OK to begin work.

On Overhead Fixtures

In nearly every single-family home, there are electrical overhead outlets in the foyer, kitchen, bedrooms, bedroom hallway, family room/kitchen,

202

and dining room. Rarely are there overhead light outlets in the living room, as this room is generally serviced only by lamps. There are overhead lights in bathrooms as well as strip lights over the medicine chests. In the case of the home that has a living room/dining room combination, there is almost always an electrical outlet in the ceiling of the dining area, over the dining-table location. When buying electrical ceiling fixtures, be certain that they are in keeping with the general scheme of your decor, in scale as well as in design. You cannot install a 36-inch-deep foyer fixture on a ceiling only eight feet two inches high. Instead, you would need a close-up fixture, one that hugs the ceiling and does not hang. I generally favor crystal close-up beaded-basket fixtures for the foyer in a traditionally decorated home. (See illustration.) These are approximately 12 inches in diameter and some six inches deep. There are a number of styles of close-up fixtures that can be

used in children's rooms, hallways, and family rooms. One of the most delightful children's-room light fixtures I have ever seen is the toy drum. The fixture is round in shape with a milklike plexiglas bottom for light diffusion. The drums come in blues, pinks, and yellows. Another children's light fixture I much admire is the hanging carousel. The carousel is available with prancing horses as well as with toy soldiers, and at very reasonable prices.

A Chandelier for the Dining Room

Chandelier light fixtures for the dining room or for the dining area in the living room/dining room combination can drop more than six or eight inches. A fixture installed over the dining table can be about 36 inches above the tabletop. Chandeliers should be hung some seven feet from the floor. There will be the times when the dining table is moved and we want to avoid accidents to the heads of family and guests, as well as to the fixture. But if your dining table will always be in place, hang the chandelier 36 inches from the top of the table. If the table is frequently moved, hang the fixture so that its bottom prism is no less than 7 feet from the floor. There are many different kinds of dining-room chandeliers to choose from —crystal prism and beaded fixtures, wood beaded fixtures, lantern fixtures. There are chandeliers of Spanish wrought-iron or Georgian brass, both with hurricane globes and shades. There are modern plexiglas ball fixtures, Tiffany-shade fixtures, wagon-wheel fixtures, and modern cylinder-shaped fixtures that hang in groups of three at staggered levels. The list is almost endless. See and examine the number of fixtures on the market and buy one that suits your fancy, your decorating ideas, and your pocketbook.

Dim for a Few Dollars

I am all for mood and atmosphere when dining. When installing your dining room chandelier, be certain to install a dimmer plate in place of the conventional wall button or snap switch. A dimmer plate with a round knob to raise and lower the intensity of your chandelier light is a great asset in creating mood for the dinner hour or for party time or cocktail hour. Dimmer plates are sold in every light-fixture store, cost less than 20 dollars, and are very easily installed. The man of the house can do the job in about ten minutes or less. All one has to do is follow the directions: unscrew the old switch plate, remove the switch, and install the new dimmer panel.

On Lamps and Lampshades

A well-lighted room will have an even distribution of light throughout the room. Note the floor plan shown in the illustration. Each lamp is so placed that the room is evenly lit. The sconces used on the wall on each side of the breakfront bring a glow of light to the right side of the room.

If you have used matching end tables, use matching lamps. If your end tables do not match, neither need your lamps. I do suggest, however, that the lamps on unmatching end tables be about the same height. End-table

lamps can be anywhere from 28½ inches high to 44 inches high, complete with shades, of course. As a rule of thumb, select end table lamps 38 inches high and you'll be safe. Do not feel restricted to using glass, china, or porcelain figure lamps. Consider lamps made from old English tea canisters, or try having a lamp made from a wine jug. There are wood lamps, wrought-iron lamps, glass lamps, ceramic lamps, porcelain lamps, plaster lamps, tin lamps, stainless-steel lamps, china lamps, marble lamps.

Nor are lampshades the big problem some people make them out to be. Somehow or other, clients and friends of mine are always bewildered when it comes to buying lampshades. They never know what size to buy. Think of a lampshade as you think of a person's head. The head starts from the neck up. The lampshade should also start from the neck up. The bottom line of the lampshade should permit the neck of the lamp to show. The shade shouldn't be placed way down over the neck of the lamp, nor should it be placed up over the neck. When it comes time to determine the height and width of the lampshade you wish to buy, first measure the height of your lamp base and lampshade holder. Include the diameter of the largest portion of your lamp base, as this will affect the top and bottom diameter measurements of the shade. Bring these measurements to your lamp store in order to make sure your shades are in proper proportion to the lamps themselves. There are many kinds of lampshades, in style as well as in

SHADE- TOO LOW   SHADE-TOO HIGH

← SHADE JUST RIGHT!

covering. There are paper accordion-pleated shades and colored-paper opaque shades that diffuse light up and down; there are translucent linen shades, vinyl translucent shades, vinyl opaque shades, silk-fabric shades. There are shades made of fabric to coordinate with a fabric used elsewhere in your room; shades made of old parchment book pages or sheet music; white shades with hand-decorated flowers, birds, or trees.

When buying lamps and lampshades, buy with an eye on three things: function, beauty, and price. Do not be taken in strictly with the novelty lamp or the novelty shade. Stick with simple lampshades and basic color shades, preferably white or off-white, or black opaque.

A Friend of mine in West Virginia decorated her Bathtub with Flowers - cut out of her coordinating wallpaper!

Chapter X

Finally

My intent in this book has been to show that a home, to be truly a home, must be created by the family as a whole. When a family works together to achieve beauty in the home, there is a sense of pride and accomplishment in the heart of every family member. My decorating philosophy for home planning and decorating can be called the "you look." The "you look" in interior design is simply the creation of a home that honestly reflects the family's personality and tastes, individually and collectively. The "you look" is an ever-growing look. During the never-ending process of growth and learning, our tastes change, our needs change, our desires change. When creating the interiors for your family home, plan the spaces around the family's personal living habits and tastes.

A family home, wherever it may be, to be comfortable, pleasant, and fun, should reflect the "you look." This does not mean in any way, however, that interior design, planning, and an awareness of styles in furnishings are to be overlooked. If this book presents planning and decorating ideas for all members of the family to think about and discuss, I have accomplished what I set out to do.

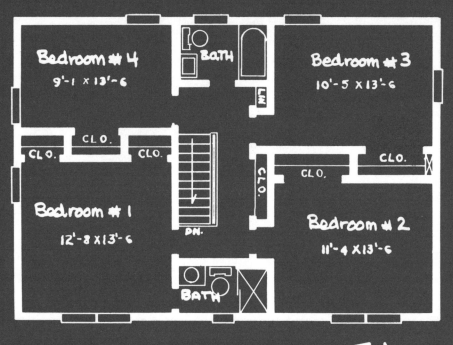

Bedroom # 4
9'-1 x 13'-6

BATH

Bedroom # 3
10'-5 x 13'-6

L.H.

CLO.

CLO.   CLO.

DN.

CLO.

CLO.   CLO.

Bedroom # 1
12'-8 x 13'-6

Bedroom # 2
11'-4 x 13'-6

BATH

Plan # 2 Upstairs

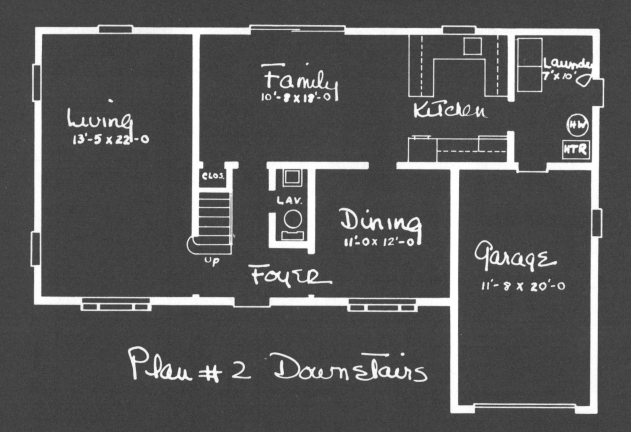

Family
10'-8 x 18'-0

Laundry
7' x 10'

Kitchen

Living
13'-5 x 22'-0

H.W.
HTR

CLOS.

LAV.

Dining
11'-0 x 12'-0

Garage
11'-8 x 20'-0

UP

Foyer

Plan # 2 Downstairs